Quiet Confidence

Breaking Up With Shyness and Silencing Self-Doubt

Joel Annesley

Quiet Confidence: Breaking Up with Shyness and Silencing Self-Doubt (Second Edition)

Copyright © Joel Annesley 2018, 2025

The moral rights of the author have been asserted.

First published in 2018 by Power Writers Publishing Group
Second edition published in 2025 by Power Writers Publishing Group

All Rights Reserved. Except as permitted under the Australian Copyright Act 1968 (for example, fair dealing for the purposes of study, research, criticism or review), no part of this book may be reproduced, stored in a retrieval system, communicated or transmitted in any form or by any means without prior written permission.

All inquiries should be directed to the author.

Disclaimer

The material in this publication is of a general nature and does not constitute professional advice. It is not intended to provide specific guidance for particular circumstances and should not be relied upon as the basis for any decision to act or not act on any matter covered. Readers should seek professional advice where appropriate before making any such decisions.

To the maximum extent permitted by law, the author and publisher disclaim all responsibility and liability for any loss or damage arising directly or indirectly from reliance on this publication.

Although every precaution has been taken to verify the information contained herein, the author assumes no responsibility for errors or omissions. No liability is accepted for any consequences arising from the use of this material.

Book cover design: Original cover design by Vanessa Maynard.
Second edition updates by Daniel Poole.
Edited by: Sarah Brown (First Edition)

ISBN: 978-1-7638925-4-5 Print
ISBN: 978-1-7638925-5-2 eBook

For more information: www.joelannesley.com

Ted Annesley, my grandfather. I never had the pleasure of knowing you, but I share your gift of Quiet Confidence.

Acknowledgments

To my family, friends, mentors, supervisors, coaches, colleagues, and clients. To those who held space when I couldn't hold it for myself, thank you.

Your belief, encouragement, and guidance made this book possible. I'm deeply grateful for every conversation, challenge, and moment of support along the way.

Foreword

Jane Turner

If only I had this book when I was a teenager!

I say that because I spent the fearful years of adolescence wishing I had a rock to crawl under because I felt humiliated about never knowing what to say. Essentially, I felt terribly inept and awkward in my own skin. This is because I lived with a debilitating mindset that played out as extreme shyness for several decades. Needless to say, it would have been wonderful to have been able to put this into the kind of perspective that a book like *Quiet Confidence* offers. At the very least, it would have been a comfort to have known that I was not alone.

I met Joel Annesley over eight years ago at one of my introductory workshops that I run to help people who want to hone their expertise and their story into a book. My own circuitous journey to becoming a published author provided me with a set of practical steps to get people started and to take them through to the truly satisfying and empowering place of completion where Joel is now.

The fact of the matter is that Joel is not the person I met eight years ago. The very best parts of him have been amplified. And the parts that stopped his light from shining on the world have diminished. I had the pleasure of watching this happen as Joel's clarity and commitment grew as he moved through the process of documenting everything that he shares with you in the following chapters.

Joel is a generous, unassuming man who has a will of steel and a commitment to making the world a better place. I am truly grateful that he signed up to work with me on his first book all those years ago. I can honestly say that I learned as much from Joel as he learned from me. The insights in this book you're reading now are uniquely Joel's, but I know they are going to resonate deeply with anyone who knows that they have a message for the world but feels stymied because they lack the self-belief that it takes to be able to speak up and assert their point of view.

Joel has beautifully crafted a roadmap for the tribe of introverted 'others' who are looking to be heard in the noisy world we live in. These are not people with vacuous ideas and white noise to add to the cluttered cultural landscape of the 21st century, but deep connectors who have been silenced to one degree or another by a culture that values extroverts over the quiet majority.

Foreword

If you take the advice that Joel provides on board, you will escape the fate that he foreshadowed when he told me that he could think of nothing worse than looking back over his life decades from now and seeing a man who lived their whole life crippled with shyness and regret. He was talking about regret for not having the guts to finally break up with shyness and start to do the things he thought would be impossible eight years ago.

I'm here to tell you that Joel has guts aplenty, and watching him emerge from lifelong habits of being a quiet and almost invisible player in the game of life to being a leader who shines the light on others who deserve more attention and satisfaction than they've had to date has been truly heart-warming for me.

It is my pleasure to welcome you to the journey to Quiet Confidence. This book presents deep and challenging material at times, and Joel has had the foresight to incorporate suggestions about times to pause and reflect on your own experience. He has also provided opportunities to communicate your thoughts to the ever-growing community that Joel brought into existence through writing his first book back in 2017.

Author's Note

There are moments in life when the person you used to be meets the person you've become. This book was born from one of those moments. It's a love letter to the part of you still waiting to believe in yourself. It's proof that quiet strength can change everything.

Welcome to your Quiet Confidence.

Introduction

We do not see things as they are, we see them as we are.

— Anaïs Nin

Who could have predicted that just a few years after launching *Quiet Confidence: Breaking Up with Shyness* alongside Jane Turner at Gleebooks, the entire world would be forced into isolation?

Overnight, life as we knew it changed. I won't dwell on the COVID years. We all carry our own scars from that time. But what's undeniable is that those years left a deep imprint, one that shaped who we are today.

In the absence of real connection, we turned to screens, reaching for the next best thing to in-person human connection. We flooded social media, searching for interaction, validation, and belonging. In doing so, we lost something. We fractured our attention spans and curated versions of ourselves, rather than simply living them. We forgot the simple, sacred art of being present with each other.

When the world opened back up, it was supposed to be a celebration. Instead, many of us felt strangely disconnected. We felt distant from others, and from ourselves. Conversations felt clumsy, and eye contact felt exposing. Being in a room full of people triggered a flutter of anxiety we couldn't quite explain. It was as if the world had finally caught up to how *you* had always felt. We had become strangers to connection, and it hurt more than we ever anticipated.

I'll admit it: at first, I didn't mind the quiet. Like many introverts, lockdown felt strangely easy, even comforting; home became a cocoon with no small talk, no overstimulation, just peace.

But eventually, the silence grew heavy. Beneath the comfort, a hollow ache whispered: You were made for connection, too. We all were.

The experience revealed something fundamental. Shyness, anxiety, and disconnection aren't just issues we struggle with. They are signs of something deeper, a hunger for authentic expression and a longing to be seen, heard, and understood.

And so, when the borders reopened and life lurched forward, we didn't just pick up where we left off. We stepped into a world that felt unfamiliar. And we weren't the same people anymore.

Introduction

For a time, I lost touch with the very mission that had inspired the first edition of this book. COVID had numbed something in me. Yes, I kept learning, growing and surviving. But somehow, the fire dimmed. The mission behind *Quiet Confidence*, the heartbeat of why I wrote it, was quietly gathering dust.

Whenever someone asked me, "Wait, didn't you write a book?"

I'd smile sheepishly. "Ah, that old thing," I'd shrug, as if I were talking about a forgotten toaster instead of something deeply valuable to me. Praise bounced off; yet any criticism stuck like glue.

But recently, during a coffee catch-up with Jane Turner, who supported me through writing the first edition and still supports me today, all these years later, something awakened in me again. She reminded me of the journey. Of the man who once stood beside her on that stage at Gleebooks, fearlessly proud and unshakably confident. And in that moment, I remembered the boy I used to be. The one who once closed his eyes and imagined a future version of himself: calm, confident and free. And there I was. I had become him.

I realised I still needed to be that support. Not just for the part of me that once struggled, but for others. For those who sit across from me in quiet rooms, sharing tears in private, feeling lost, confused, and isolated, unsure of where to turn. Reconnecting with this gave me a renewed sense of purpose. A duty to help. A calling I could no longer ignore.

Here's something I've come to understand. Not just through my own journey, but in my clinical work too. Healing often begins

Introduction

the moment the problem stops being the centre of your world. When you are no longer caught in it, but gently turning toward something greater: your future, your strengths, your possibilities.

That's when the shift becomes visible. When you stop gripping so tightly to what was wrong, and begin quietly living your way into something better. Often, my clients don't even realise how far they've come until I reflect it back to them. I remind them of where they began, and who they are now. And in doing so, I remember why I do this work. That gives me meaning.

What I've come to see is, so many people are struggling. More than they let on. They're living with anxiety that no one sees. Doubting themselves. Hiding their voice, their needs, their brilliance. Maybe they've forgotten who they are. Or maybe they never had the chance to truly know it.

That realisation moved through me like a wave. Quiet Confidence was never outdated. If anything, it's more needed now than ever. Because today, it's not just about breaking up with shyness. It's about silencing self-doubt and stepping into who you were always meant to be.

In the years since its first release, the world has changed. So have I. So has this book. And I'd bet, in your own way, so have you.

This 2025 edition of *Quiet Confidence: Breaking Up with Shyness and Silencing Self-Doubt* isn't a rewrite. It's a renaissance. It's been expanded, reworked, and reimagined with the wisdom, experience, and tenderness that only time and

Introduction

adversity can bring. It's the same heart, expressed with new depth. The same spirit, grounded in greater clarity.

Just like Gleebooks, newly renovated yet still holding the soul of what made it beloved, this book too has evolved. Quietly, yet confidently. Now it's your turn, because here's the truth.

If you've ever felt shy, anxious, disconnected, or small in a world that demands you to be loud to be seen, this book isn't just for you; it *is* you. It's the gentle nudge you didn't know you needed and the reminder that there is nothing wrong with you. It's time to come home to yourself.

So wherever you're starting from, whether you're clinging to your comfort zone, quietly doubting your worth, or simply tired of feeling stuck, know this: you're not alone, and you never were.

Today, the message runs deeper than shyness. This is about silencing self-doubt and stepping fully into the person you were always meant to be.

The Quiet Battle That Shaped Me

This is a story about finally breaking free from the patterns that kept you small. It's about the quiet battle so many of us fight in silence. The one between who we are and who we believe we're allowed to be.

For me, that battle was called shyness. It shaped everything. How I spoke, or didn't. How I showed up. What I believed was possible. Left unchecked, it became toxic. I spent years

Introduction

imagining a future version of myself who had the confidence to live fully, even though that kind of life felt out of reach. But I also feared waking up decades later with nothing but regret. Regret for not speaking up in the very moments when my heart was urging me to speak my truth. Regret for letting fear and self-doubt stop me in my tracks, making me feel small. At one point, the fear of regret became stronger than the fear itself. Stronger than the pull of shyness. The thought of looking back and wondering what could have been became more unbearable than the discomfort of showing up. That was the turning point.

This book is the story of what happened when I stopped waiting. When I stopped trying to fix myself and instead built a new relationship; with my mind, my body, and my voice. It's a story of breaking up with shyness, yes, but also of silencing the self-doubt that had been quietly shaping my life for far too long.

There was no single breakthrough. No overnight transformation. Just a turning point. A quiet decision to allow myself to grow. From there, the shifts began. Gentle at first, then stronger. With each step, a new possibility opened, and with it, the growing realisation that maybe, just maybe, I was already enough.

If Shyness Didn't Hold You Back...

This journey sparked a mission within me: to help as many introverts as possible break up with shyness, silence self-doubt, and step into their Quiet Confidence. Maybe you're one of them. Maybe someone close to you is. Either way, the insights in this book will serve you in ways you may not yet realise.

Introduction

So let me ask you: how would your life be different if shyness no longer held you back?

For many years, I believed shyness was me. It was woven into my identity. I was too shy to speak up in class, to answer the phone, to use the urinal, to make friends. But here's what changed everything.

I stopped trying to fix it and started to listen. I began to wonder what it was protecting me from. And in that quiet questioning, I uncovered something powerful: shyness wasn't who I was; it was how I stayed safe.

Once I really grasped this concept, everything began to shift. Now I have the opportunity to share this with you.

I don't know what you look like, but I have a good idea of how your mind works. If I had to guess, we have a lot in common. We're empathic and highly sensitive introverts who feel everything deeply and think even deeper. It's a beautiful human quality. But sometimes, that depth turns into overthinking, and instead of clarity, we find ourselves spinning. We become anxious, overwhelmed, and unsure where to place our next step. We wrestle with self-doubt, second-guessing ourselves into inaction. And most of the time, we suffer in silence.

But not anymore. This book is about addressing the uncomfortable. It won't always be easy. At times, we'll face some ugly characters: fear, self-doubt, social anxiety, that relentless inner critic. It might stir things up. It might even feel turbulent. But on the other side of that discomfort is something extraordinary: a new way of seeing yourself and your place in the world.

At the heart of this journey is Quiet Confidence. And once you discover it, nothing will ever be the same again.

Becoming the Person I Once Needed

This book isn't just about breaking up with shyness. It's about rewriting the story you tell yourself.

How? By learning to master that voice inside your head; the one that whispers, or sometimes shouts, self-doubt, hesitation, and fear. The one that keeps your lips sealed when you want to speak. You'll learn how to quiet that voice, regain control, and begin seeing yourself in a whole new light. The more you step into this mindset, the calmer, more grounded, and less dependent on outside validation you'll become. This shift alone can change everything.

If you've struggled with shyness, if your mind is a maze of overthinking, this book offers an opportunity to change your life. But you have to be open to it. That's a big ask, I know. But my story is proof. Clear evidence that shyness isn't a life sentence. And when you learn to silence the self-doubt that fuels it, you set yourself free. For me, finding Quiet Confidence was like being handed a get-out-of-jail-free card. It wasn't an overnight shift, but it was the most valuable journey I've ever taken. I wouldn't trade it for anything.

The way I see myself has completely changed. I no longer beat myself up. I speak to myself with the kind of kindness I used to

Introduction

reserve for everyone else. The things I once saw as weaknesses have become my greatest strengths. Now, as a confidence coach and hypnotherapist, I witness breakthrough moments of Quiet Confidence every day. Small, consistent, quiet actions over time have allowed me to create workshops, build transformative programs, and connect with thousands of people like you. I've done it all without pretending to be an extrovert or forcing myself to be someone I'm not.

Here's what I've learned. The more I follow my heart, the more life-changing opportunities find me.

I used to envy confident people. I thought they had something I lacked. I confused extroversion with confidence and assumed I'd always be behind. I was wrong. Today, I live a life I once thought was impossible. I've made the impossible probable. One day soon, I hope you'll tell me the same.

Not Louder, Just Stronger

This isn't a book about teaching you how to be more extroverted; it won't offer scripts for small talk or tricks to fake being outgoing, because confidence isn't about putting on a show. It's about showing up fully, quietly, authentically, and with presence.

This is a book about embracing who you already are and evolving into a version of yourself you haven't yet discovered. It's not about changing into someone you're not. It's about uncovering a quiet, unshakable confidence in yourself and your abilities. It's about stepping up, not to be louder, but to be stronger. To live a life powered by purpose and no longer paralysed by fear.

Why should you commit to this book?

I'm not here to convince you. I'm here to share my story: the wins, struggles and the raw truths. And to invite you to pause, reflect, and begin your own.

Because this won't be a passive experience. Breaking up with shyness and stepping into Quiet Confidence isn't something that happens just by reading a few inspiring words. It's a decision, a practice, and an inner evolution that reshapes how you show up in the world.

And I want you to know, I'm with you every step of the way.

As you read, you'll likely see pieces of your own story reflected in mine. Let this book feel familiar. Like an old friend who understands your fears but also sees your greatness. A friend who won't let you settle for less than you deserve.

Let it feel like a love letter, speaking to the part of you still waiting to believe in yourself.

I'm not a doctor, a researcher, or a psychologist. I'm not here to diagnose or prescribe a one-size-fits-all fix. What I offer is grounded in lived experience, years of studying the field, deep personal reflection, and walking alongside countless number of clients on their own path to Quiet Confidence.

At times, this book might stir something inside you. You may

Introduction

feel challenged. You may feel emotional. If that happens, it's not a sign you're doing it wrong. It's a sign you're waking up.

If anything feels overwhelming, take a moment to reflect. Let the words settle. And if something rises that feels too heavy to carry alone, please seek support. That might be through working with me, or someone else you trust. You don't have to walk this path alone.

Now, take a deep breath. Quietly, yet confidently...

Let's begin.

Chapter 1

The Identity Trap: Why Shyness Feels Like Who You Are (But Isn't)

"You are not the labels they give you. You are the story you choose to believe."

— *Unknown*

Mistaken Identity

I used to believe shyness defined who I was. It wasn't just a feeling; it was my identity. It dictated how I moved through the world, a silent force shaping every decision, every interaction, every missed opportunity. If someone called me shy, I didn't question it. I accepted it and wore it like a name tag.

Maybe you have felt the same way. Perhaps you've spent years avoiding situations because you identified as shy. Maybe you've turned down invitations, stayed quiet in conversations, or shrunk into the background because it felt safer. Maybe you have watched confident people and thought, I could never be like that. Confidence belongs to them, not me.

You Weren't Always Shy

You were never born shy; you were born curious. You came into this world open, expressive, and making noise without fear of judgement. That natural boldness didn't disappear; it was shaped, redirected, and misunderstood. Over time, what you experienced taught you to hold back.

Shyness isn't who you are. It's something you learned: a reaction, a habit, a pattern so practised it started to feel permanent. But it's not. You can break the pattern. You can silence self-doubt. And you can rediscover the Quiet Confidence that has always lived inside you.

How Shyness Takes Hold

We're not born afraid to be seen. We come into the world trusting we'll be held; reaching, exploring, expressing without shame. We lock eyes with strangers, wide with unfiltered wonder. We cry out when we need something, with no hesitation, no second-guessing.

Then, something changes. For me, it started in childhood. I was an observant, quiet child, deeply tuned into the emotions of those around me. My parents described me as an empathic and sensitive child, one of those types who didn't always have the words, but felt everything. I wasn't loud, but I was deeply curious.

I would sit quietly next to my grandmother as she practised floral art, the art of arranging flowers. It was her creative expression, and one in which I took a keen interest. I made miniature installations using moss collected from the nearby creek beds on our eighty-acre property. I would add flowers, rocks, and stones.

I was a child of nature, exploring and discovering local swimming spots and waterfalls. I lived in a land of imagination, where the boundary between the imaginary and the physical world blurred.

Gradually, my curiosity gave way to caution. The world started to feel less safe to explore. Others saw my quietness and called it shyness, so I did too.

The Moment I Learned Silence Was Safer

I was five years old when I learned that speaking up could be dangerous. Sitting at my desk, my fingers curled around my pencil so tightly they ached. My teacher's voice cut through the room like a whip: sharp, cold and unforgiving.

I could feel her gaze sweep across the classroom, searching for her next victim. My breath caught in my throat as I hunched down, making myself smaller, hoping she wouldn't see me.

"Joel. What's three plus four?"

A heavy drop sank in my stomach as my mind emptied completely, leaving only a blur where thoughts used to be. My heartbeat roared in my ears, steady and relentless, like a drumbeat I couldn't silence.

I knew the answer, but the words got stuck. There was a disconnection between my mind and my voice, as if the signal never made it to my vocal cords. I was frozen, experiencing a sensation I had never felt before.

"Joel."

I opened my mouth, but what came out wasn't clear. A blur of sound—half-formed, shaky, almost inaudible.

"Wrong!" she snapped. Her voice was sharp, laced with anger.

A jolt of shame surged through my chest. My shoulders tensed. My whole body pulled inward. I wanted to disappear. To sink into the floor, to fade into the furniture. I remember thinking, with every cell in my body *Get me out of here*.

That was the moment I learned a dangerous lesson. Not that I didn't know the answer, but that even when I did, trying to speak it could still go wrong. I learned that getting it wrong, or sounding unsure, could invite humiliation. That silence, though painful, was safer than exposure.

So I stayed quiet.

Hiding in Plain Sight

Shyness isn't just about not talking. It's about hiding. By the time I was seven, I had perfected the art of disappearing in plain sight. I could sit in a classroom full of kids and be completely invisible. I could walk through a playground without drawing a single glance. I avoided anything that might make me the centre of attention.

When the bell rang for recess, I wouldn't race outside like the other kids. Instead, I would sit in the lunchroom, head down, quietly eating my peanut butter sandwich while everyone else rushed off to play. I wouldn't move until the last possible second.

Even then, I wouldn't go straight to the playground. I'd take my time, circling the edges, watching from a distance.

I wasn't just a shy kid; I was a ghost. And the worst part was, I hated it. It goes without saying, I wanted to join in. I wanted to laugh, to play, to belong. But the moment I considered stepping forward, the voice in my head spoke up.

You'll look stupid. They don't want you there. You'll say something dumb. You don't belong.

So I stayed on the sidelines. Again and again.

The Evidence That Shaped Me

The tricky thing about shyness is that it starts as a feeling, but it quickly becomes proof of who you are.

At the end of the school term, my report card came home. Under Social Growth and Work Habits, my teacher had written:

Joel is very reserved and nervous in new or unfamiliar situations and needs time to adjust and gain confidence. He prefers to watch his classmates at play rather than to join in.

There it was. In black and white. A label that confirmed everything I feared. I wasn't just imagining it. I really was different. Other kids played effortlessly, and I watched. Other kids jumped into new situations, and I needed time to adjust.

What I didn't realise then was just how much weight I would place on that statement. It wasn't simply an observation from a teacher; it became something I absorbed as truth. To me, it was proof. Proof that I was shy. Proof that I wasn't like everyone else, that I didn't belong in the centre of the action. Proof that I would always be on the outside looking in, quietly watching life unfold rather than stepping fully into it.

And once I accepted that belief, I started seeing evidence of it everywhere.

The Growing Divide

At first, I didn't know why I felt different. In time, my confidence started to grow, and shyness took a slight reprieve. I made my first real friends in the sandpit at lunch, building worlds out of sticks and stones.

But even then, something nagged at me.

I desperately wanted to know what it felt like to fit in. Even though I was learning to make friends, this thought plagued me.

Instead of focusing on what I was gaining, I became fixated on what made me different.

The more I focused on my differences, the shyer and more isolated I felt. The more I convinced myself I didn't belong.

One of the biggest differences I clung to was that I was a year older than my classmates. Kids would ask why I wasn't their age, and every time, a wave of embarrassment would hit me.

I didn't know how to explain it, so I said, "I was kept back."

Kept back. As if I had failed.

The truth was, my parents had pulled me out of school because it wasn't the right fit. I hadn't failed anything. I had done well academically.

But that's not what I told myself. I took this one difference and turned it into proof that I was slow. That I wasn't smart enough. That I was falling behind.

And that's when another belief took root.

I'm slow. I'm not smart enough. It must mean I'm a failure.

But isn't it interesting. That's what I focused on. While my mind was busy collecting evidence of why I didn't belong, what wasn't I paying attention to?

The One Place I Felt Free

During lunchtime, I would stretch out on the carpet, close my eyes, and daydream. It was my escape.

I would picture myself miles away from where I was. I wasn't the shy kid anymore. I was someone else, somewhere else. In those moments, I felt happy, safe, free.

There was only one other place I felt that way: art class.

It was the only class where I didn't feel like I had to prove myself. The only place where there were no wrong answers. No right or wrong way to do things. Just me and creative expression.

Unlike my regular teacher, my art teacher was warm and encouraging. She praised my work and told me I had talent. But isn't it interesting? That's not what I focused on.

I focused on the belief that I wasn't enough, that I was different, and that I didn't belong. And with that, my first real negative belief system about school was born.

School is not a safe place for me. It's best I keep quiet to avoid being ridiculed.

And that belief followed me for years.

Breaking the Illusion: Shyness Is Learned, Not Who You Are

Let me ask you something. What happens when you stop calling yourself shy?

Seriously. What if, from this moment on, you stopped using the word entirely? What if you saw it not as who you are, but as something you've experienced?

You were never meant to be a gazelle, running from fear. You were born a lion. But when you're constantly told you're small, you start to believe it. And when you believe it long enough, you forget you were ever anything else.

The shift starts here.

Shyness isn't a life sentence; it's a learned response. And that means it can be unlearned.

The Truth About Shyness and the Self-Doubt Beneath It

Looking back, it's clear that my struggle with shyness wasn't just about being quiet. It was about where my focus was.

I had been so focused on what made me different that I couldn't see where I belonged. I had been so fixated on avoiding embarrassment that I didn't allow myself to take even small risks. I was so caught up in proving my fears right that I ignored the evidence that suggested otherwise.

When my school report card described me as reserved and nervous, I took it as proof that something was wrong with me. But I didn't pay attention to the fact that, over time, I had started to make friends. I didn't focus on the moments where I was creative, expressive, and completely free in art class.

When kids asked why I was a year older, I focused on the idea that I was slow, even though I had never actually failed. I ignored the truth. I had been removed from an environment that didn't serve me. I was capable. I was learning at my own pace.

That's what the shyness response does. It narrows your focus and invites in self-doubt. It turns every quiet moment into evidence that you are small, that you are different, that you are not enough.

But what if I had trained my focus differently? What if, instead of looking for ways I didn't fit in, I had looked for moments where I did? What if I had paid attention to the encouragement I received instead of the judgement I feared?

Shyness isn't just about hesitation or social discomfort. It's about the stories you tell yourself and the ones you choose to believe.

For years, I told myself I wasn't smart enough, fast enough, or confident enough. And because I focused so much on those thoughts, they felt real. But in reality, they were just a distorted perception: a version of the world shaped by fear, not fact.

Here's what I want you to take away from this: Shyness isn't who you are. It's something you learned: a nervous system response shaped by experience; a habit of protection, often fuelled by self-doubt, and practised so often it starts to feel permanent.

Quietly, yet confidently, you can begin to see yourself differently. And when you do, everything changes. Let this chapter be the beginning of something new: a quiet awakening. A return to the version of you that still believes in possibility. That part of you was never lost, just waiting for the right invitation. Maybe, just maybe, this is it.

Key Takeaways from Chapter One

- **Shyness is not your identity.** It's something you learned, and anything learned can be unlearned.
- **Labels become self-fulfilling.** A single comment, report, or experience can shape how we see ourselves. But we don't have to keep wearing those labels.
- **The moment you felt different didn't mean something was wrong with you.** More often, it meant those around you didn't understand your quiet strength.
- **Avoidance becomes a habit**. Shyness reinforces itself through withdrawal, hesitation, and fear of judgement until it starts to feel permanent.
- **Your focus shapes your reality**. When you focus only on what makes you feel small, you overlook the evidence of your strengths. Change your focus, and you change your story.
- **You were born curious, expressive, and open.** That version of you still exists, buried beneath layers of fear. This book will help you reclaim it.
- **You can begin again, quietly yet confidently.** Power doesn't come from being loud. It comes from refusing to believe the story that says you aren't enough.

Chapter 2

More Than a Label: Reclaiming Who You Really Are

"It ain't what they call you, it's what you answer to."

— *W.C. Fields*

The Labels We Wear

Labels. They have the power to build you up or tear you down. They can be a source of belonging or a weapon of exclusion. A single label can define how others see you. And worse, how you see yourself. Some labels we choose. Others feel as though they've been placed upon us. And some, once accepted, shape the very foundation of our identity. Sometimes for the better. Sometimes for the worse.

I spent years unknowingly collecting labels, absorbing them like a sponge, never questioning if they truly belonged to me. Quiet. Shy.

Different. Weird. Strange. Outsider. I didn't just wear them; I carried them like a weight, letting them dictate who I was and who I could become. But one label had the power to change everything; not just by offering clarity, but by breaking through the confusion.

It helped me reframe some of those old labels in a different light, make sense of a few, reject others, and even accept parts I hadn't yet understood. And yet, it brought with it a whole new layer of uncertainty.

When You Don't Know Where You Belong

I stared at my own reflection, searching for something, clarity or certainty. What I was looking for was permission to exist in a way that made sense. But the world I saw didn't translate to the world I felt. All I saw was confusion. Who was I? The questions swirled, relentless. My body told me things my mind couldn't understand. I felt different, but different how?

During the day, I distracted myself. I laughed when I was supposed to, spoke when necessary, and avoided any situation that might force me to confront what I already knew deep down. But at night, when the house was quiet and there was no one to perform for, I couldn't escape it. I lay awake, anxiety gripping my chest, whispering the same terrifying question over and over: *What if I never belong?*

I was suffocating under the weight of my own thoughts, yet I couldn't find the words to release them. Even if I could, who would I tell? Who could possibly understand? The loneliness was unbearable. I wanted answers. But more than that, I wanted to exhale.

My father must have sensed something because one evening, he handed me the car keys.

"Let's go for a drive."

I was preparing for my driver's licence test, so the more experience, the better. I nodded, grateful for the distraction, but the road ahead felt heavier than usual.

We drove in silence, the air thick with unspoken words. The car rumbled up to the local lookout point, the town stretching below us in the fading light. I put the handbrake on, my fingers gripping the wheel like a lifeline. My heart pounded. I wasn't ready for this conversation, but the truth was clawing its way out whether I liked it or not.

"You know you can talk to me about anything," my father said gently. "There isn't anything you're going through that I haven't."

I wanted to believe him, but he was wrong. He had never been in my shoes. He didn't know what it was like to feel like an outsider in your own body. He had never had to question if he would still be loved for being exactly who he was.

My stomach twisted.

"What is it, Joel?" he pressed.

I swallowed hard.

"I'm different."

"Different how?"

My throat closed up. I wanted to say it. *Dad, I'm gay.*

But the words stuck. Saying it out loud would make it real. Saying it out loud meant there was no going back. I had played this moment over in my head a thousand times, but now that it was here, I was paralysed.

The silence stretched.

He looked at me, as if trying to read what I couldn't say.

"Is it about who you're attracted to?"

I nodded, feeling the heat rise in my face. I wanted to disappear.

"Are you... asexual?"

I almost laughed at the absurdity. "No."

He paused. "Do you feel attracted to guys?"

There it was. The moment of truth. I nodded again, barely able to look at him.

A million thoughts raced through my mind. *What will he think? Will he still talk to me? Will he reject me? Will he still love me?*

He reached over and placed a hand on my shoulder.

"I love you, my son. Nothing will ever change that."

And just like that, I exhaled. The tension, the fear, the crippling self-doubt. It didn't disappear, but for the first time in a long time, I felt lighter.

The Hidden Question Behind Every Label

Coming out isn't something everyone goes through. But for those of us who don't fit the definition of straight, it's not just a moment. It's a reckoning.

It sounds like a statement, *I'm gay*, but underneath, it's a question.

Will you still love me? Will I still belong?

For some, the answer is silence. Or distance. Or a slammed door. Some are disowned. Others never speak the words aloud at all because they already know what the answer would be.

I was lucky. My dad didn't flinch. My family loved me, no questions, no hesitation. But even in their love, there was a part of me that stayed uncertain. Because the truth is, even when others accept you, it doesn't mean you've accepted yourself.

I thought naming it would fix it; if I could just say the words, *I'm gay*, everything would make sense. That the shame would lift. That the shyness and self-doubt would fade. That I'd finally feel like me.

But it didn't happen that way. Because coming out gave me a label, but it didn't give me peace. It answered one question, but not the bigger one.

Not the one I'd been carrying my whole life.

But what happens when the labels you're given don't reflect who you really are? What if they only capture part of you, or worse, misrepresent you entirely?

Do you shrink to fit them? Do you spend your life trying to escape them? Or do you learn to rewrite them, on your own terms?

Just because I was gay didn't mean I suddenly fit the mould I saw around me. I didn't become a scene queen overnight. I wasn't drawn to drag, didn't want to dance on podiums or become every woman's shopping bestie. The only real reference I had at the time was the 1994 film *Priscilla, Queen of the Desert* — while parts I found entertaining, it also made me wonder if that's what I had to become in order to be seen.

I didn't see myself in the stereotypes, but I didn't know where else I belonged. And long before I ever found the words, the world had already handed me its version of who I was.

Wear Your Labels. Don't Let Them Wear You

Before I could reclaim anything, I had to face what I'd absorbed... all those years ago. I was taken back to the playground. Insults dressed up as jokes.

"That's so gay."

Gay meant stupid. And that wasn't the only insult. Back then, I didn't even fully understand what the words meant. But I knew how they made me feel: humiliated, exposed, wrong. I didn't know who I was yet, but the world had already decided I was something to laugh at.

So I went quiet. In high school, even when I found the courage to share my newfound pride with close friends, I still kept parts of myself hidden, even from myself. I didn't feel safe. Because when you grow up hearing your identity used as an insult, it doesn't just sting; it buries itself deep. It shapes how you walk into a room, how you hold your body, how you speak. Or don't.

I left school, left home, and came out; but those words still echoed. But something changed. I stopped hearing those labels through someone else's shame. I started hearing them through my own power. I didn't just accept them; I rewrote them. I reclaimed them, not just as labels, but as truth, wholeness, freedom.

That's the power of language: it can define you, or it can liberate you. And once you decide what your labels mean, no one else gets to hold that power over you. The moment I stopped letting those words shame me, I started letting them shape me. But this time, on my terms.

The Anthem That Changed Everything

If there's one person who embodies that spirit, it's Lady Gaga. She didn't just wear her labels; she redefined them. She turned "freak" into "fabulous," "different" into "divine." Her art became a declaration: *You don't need to become someone else to be worthy. You were already born enough.*

When I first heard *Born This Way*, it hit me like a tidal wave. I wasn't just singing along; I was hearing the words my younger self had needed for years.

> "Don't hide yourself in regret
> Just love yourself and you're set
> I'm on the right track, baby
> I was born this way."

Those words didn't ask for permission. They didn't wait for approval. They were an affirmation.

Love yourself. You're already on the right track. You were born this way.

That was the moment it clicked: I didn't need to fit a mould to feel proud. I didn't need to prove anything or edit myself to be accepted. I could choose what my labels meant. I could belong without bending. And so can you.

The Labels That Shape Us (And How to Break Free)

Sometimes, it takes time to gain perspective, to realise that identity isn't a performance; it's a process. A process of choosing what's true for you and gently letting go of what no longer fits. I embraced the pride of being a gay man, but I also realised I didn't have to live up to every stereotype that came with it. That was the gift: choice. The understanding that sexuality is just one part of who I am, not the whole story.

There is so much more to you than any single label could ever capture. For me, one of the most empowering shifts came when I embraced another label, one I had misunderstood for years: *Introvert.*

For years, I mistook introversion for shyness, as so many people do. I believed that being quiet meant I was timid, socially inept, or lacking confidence. But in reality, introversion has nothing to do with shyness.

Shyness is born from a lack of self-confidence and fear of ridicule. In my case, it latched onto the young boy who didn't have confidence in himself or his abilities after being belittled by his first-grade teacher. The experience cemented the idea that speaking up was risky and that silence was safer. Over time, this belief became my reality. I wore shyness like armour, mistaking it for part of my identity.

Introversion, on the other hand, is a tremendous gift that allows for inquisitive curiosity about life. Introversion created in this young boy a fascination with nature, science, creativity, and imagination. I would sit for hours, watching the way sunlight filtered through the trees, collecting moss and rocks to create miniature landscapes.

My introversion gave me the ability to observe, to reflect, and to see details others overlooked.

Introvert, Not Invisible

What does it actually mean to be an introvert? It's not about being shy or socially awkward. It's about how you gain energy. Introverts recharge in solitude, while extroverts thrive in social settings. If you've ever felt drained after a long day of socialising, that's not shyness. That's just your introverted nature needing time to reset.

For a long time, society has celebrated extroversion. The loudest voices in the room get the attention. The people who speak up quickly and dominate conversations. Who are comfortable in the spotlight. These people are seen as natural leaders. But that's a narrow, outdated view of confidence. Confidence isn't about being the loudest in the room. It's about knowing who you are and owning it.

You Define You

At some point, I realised that I was letting labels choose me instead of the other way around. I let the world tell me I was shy. I let teachers, classmates, and social norms dictate how I was supposed to be.

But the moment I chose my own labels, everything changed. I wasn't shy; I was an observer. I wasn't awkward; I was thoughtful and intentional. I wasn't weak; I was quietly resilient. And most importantly, I wasn't a failure. I was simply still learning to embrace who I was.

Quiet Doesn't Mean Weak

One of the biggest myths I believed was that confidence and extroversion were the same thing: that in order to be confident, I had to be the one speaking the most, standing in the spotlight, radiating energy. But confidence isn't about volume. It's about how you see yourself, how you carry yourself, and how comfortable you are in the quiet.

Some of the most powerful people in the world are introverts. They don't need to be the loudest. Their confidence comes from knowing who they are. They don't seek validation. They don't try to prove anything. They just show up fully, as themselves.

When I stopped trying to force myself into extroverted spaces and started honouring my natural strengths, everything changed. My confidence didn't come from being louder; it came from being comfortable in my own skin.

Own Who You Are And Watch Everything Change

For most of my life, I questioned who I was. I analysed every interaction, every moment of hesitation, every time I felt like an outsider. But the moment I stopped questioning and started owning my identity, things began to shift.

When you stop seeing your quiet nature as a flaw and start recognising it as a strength, you begin to move differently. You stop feeling the need to overcompensate. You stop trying to prove yourself. You start embracing your unique way of showing up in the world.

There's no need to reinvent yourself or become someone you're not. You can choose to reconnect with the version of you who exists beyond the noise of self-doubt. Because that part of you never left. They've just been waiting for you to remember. When you do that, when you quietly and confidently own who you are, the world takes notice.

Key Takeaways from Chapter Two

- **You are not your label.** Labels can help you make sense of your experience, but they should never determine your worth.
- **Language shapes your reality, until you reclaim it and rewrite what it means to you.** Words that once felt like shame can become sources of truth, strength, and identity... if you choose to reclaim them.
- **Shyness and introversion are not the same.** Shyness is shaped by fear and self-doubt, while introversion is about where you draw your energy, often from solitude and depth rather than external stimulation.
- **You get to define who you are.** If a label empowers you, keep it. If it limits you, let it go. You're not here to fit into someone else's box.
- **Confidence doesn't come from performing.** It begins the moment you stop trying to prove your worth and start standing in it.
- **Your quiet nature is not a weakness.** It's a strength. When you honour it instead of hiding it, you make room for your Quiet Confidence to thrive.

Chapter 3

Unfreezing the Freeze: Shyness, Self-Doubt, and the Power to Choose

"Between stimulus and response there is a space. In that space is our power to choose our response."

— *Viktor E. Frankl*

The Fear Beneath the Quiet

You knew the answer. Your hand could have gone up, and you could have spoken. A part of you even wanted to, but you didn't. You sat there, holding it in, silently praying the teacher would call on someone else, hoping the moment would pass before your heart beat its way right through your chest and onto the floor where everyone could see it. You told yourself it wasn't worth the risk, that someone else could say it better, that it wasn't important anyway.

Quiet Confidence

What you were really saying was: *I'm not enough. I'll mess it up. They'll judge me.*

That's the part we don't always see. Behind the stillness is a storm (one we will return to in Chapter 11). Not just fear, but self-doubt whispering that you don't belong in the spotlight. That your voice will expose something shameful or inadequate.

I carried that same pattern like an invisible weight for years. From the classroom to the workplace. From speaking in meetings to making small talk at lunch. I learned to stay quiet, even in the moments when my thoughts felt most important—especially then. Silence became my survival strategy.

And that's what shyness becomes: *survival.*

We're taught to think of shyness as a personality trait, something fixed and unchangeable. Something you're either born with or cursed with. But it's not. Shyness is a response. It's not who you are; it's how your nervous system learned to protect you. At its core, shyness is a form of avoidance. It's the body's way of saying, let's not risk it. Let's stay safe. Let's stay small.

But staying small doesn't feel safe forever. At some point, it starts to feel suffocating.

Beneath the hesitation is fear: fear of being judged, of being wrong, of being exposed. But also, fear of being seen and not measuring up. That's the part self-doubt adds to the mix: the belief that even if you do show up, you won't be enough.

That fear doesn't come from nowhere. It's the product of moments where you were hurt, dismissed, misunderstood, or humiliated—moments that taught you that being visible is dangerous.

But how true are those thoughts today? Are they really valid? Just because something once hurt you doesn't mean it will again.

The past may have shaped your reflexes, but it doesn't get to write your future. And awareness is where that rewriting begins.

How Shyness Shows Up

Shyness isn't always obvious. It doesn't just live in blushing cheeks or a quiet voice. It hides in moments, in decisions, in the ways we hold ourselves back without even realising it. Sometimes it shows up when you walk into a room full of strangers and feel yourself shrinking, your mind scanning for the nearest exit. That's shyness responding to the unfamiliar.

Sometimes it rises when you need to perform, speak, or be seen. Your voice trembles, your mind blanks, your hands sweat. That's shyness responding to pressure.

And sometimes, it's not a moment; it's a mindset. A quiet narrative whispering that this is just who you are, that you'll always feel this way, that you'll never change.

That third version? That's the one I carried for years.

If you've been reading this far, you've seen how shyness once felt like my identity; not something I experienced, but something I *was*. Quiet, reserved, always one step back.

But what I've come to understand, and what you're beginning to explore, is that shyness isn't who you are. It's something you *feel* in certain moments, something that can shift, soften, and lose its grip once you learn to see it for what it really is.

Shyness Is the Freeze Response in Disguise

Shyness isn't a flaw. It's your nervous system's attempt to keep you safe from what it perceives as a threat. We don't call it that, of course. We call it being "reserved," "soft-spoken," "introverted," or "just a bit shy." But what's really happening is that your body is reacting as if you're in danger, even when you're simply trying to speak in a meeting or introduce yourself at a party.

This isn't about actual danger. It's about perceived danger, especially the kind that stems from fearing how you might be judged. When your nervous system becomes hyper-attuned to how you're being perceived, even neutral situations can feel threatening. The moment your brain senses potential disapproval or rejection, the freeze response kicks in. You hesitate. You hold back. And over time, perceived judgment becomes the cue for avoidance.

Your system does what it was designed to do. It protects you. When the alert for possible judgement starts flashing, your mind and body respond automatically. They tell you to retreat, to shrink, to disappear. It's not a flaw; it's a learned response. Your brain made the connection that being seen might lead to pain, and ever since, it's been trying to protect you from that risk.

It's a brilliant system. But it's running on outdated data. And here's where it gets even trickier: the freeze response doesn't feel like a reaction. It feels like you. You don't just feel shy; you believe you are shy. The self-doubt, the critical voice whispering judgement? It feels like truth. Like identity. But it's not. It's a habit. A pattern. A protective strategy etched into your nervous system.

Even more painful, the freeze isn't usually in response to something that's actually happening. It's preparing for something that might. It's protecting you from a story; one you've often repeated silently to yourself for years.

They'll laugh. You'll get it wrong. They'll think you're stupid. You're not good enough.

Those thoughts aren't grounded in the moment. They're predictions, shaped by past pain and fuelled by your brain's negativity bias. And, like most fear-based forecasts, they're far more likely to be wrong than right.

A Freeze Moment That Changed Everything

I've experienced the freeze response more times than I can count. One moment in particular has stayed with me. I don't revisit it with heaviness, but with a quiet sense of recognition. Something shifted that day. A subtle turning point that helped me begin to see what was really going on underneath.

I was in a team meeting. There was space to contribute, but I stayed silent. I told myself I didn't have anything worthwhile to add. But beneath that surface excuse was a deeper fear. If I spoke and it didn't land, if I stumbled or showed hesitation, people might realise I wasn't as capable as they thought.

So I froze. I listened. I judged myself. And the longer I waited, the heavier the silence became.

Eventually, I forced myself to speak.

The words came out fast, clumsy... I rambled. My rambling clearly wasn't to contribute something meaningful, because the reality was... I was just trying to outrun the rising shame. That inner voice had convinced me that if I stayed quiet a second longer, the judgement would be even harsher.

Later that day, I realised something I still carry with me:

Just because you're in the room doesn't mean you need to speak.

There's no invisible scoreboard. You don't need to perform to earn your place. And you certainly don't need to abandon your own pace just to prove your worth.

Choosing silence doesn't have to mean shame. Sometimes, it's an act of self-trust. It's giving yourself permission to breathe, to process, to reflect. Your most powerful thoughts might not come in the moment, and that's okay. Maybe they'll come after. Maybe they'll come when you're alone. Maybe others will simply need to learn and adapt to how you work.

The Unlearning Begins

Here's the quiet truth that changed everything for me: shyness is not a fixed trait. It is not your personality. It is a response your body and mind learned over time, often without you realising. And what has been learned can be gently unlearned.

There is nothing missing in you. No secret ingredient everyone else was handed. What you have carried is a nervous system that adapted to protect you in the only way it knew how: by holding back, by staying small, by looking for danger even in safe moments. But your world has changed, and so have you. You are no longer that child. You have more support now, more tools to work with, more choice in how you respond, and more strength than you probably give yourself credit for.

What if your voice is not a liability, but a gift? What if being seen isn't dangerous but freeing? What if confidence isn't something you perform, but something you remember?

Shyness is a signal. It's your body asking, am I safe here? It's your mind saying, I don't want to be judged.

The answer isn't to fight it; it's to meet it. To recognise it for what it is—a protective pattern—and respond with presence, with compassion, and with a gentle reminder: I am safe now. I can choose where I place my focus. This is how your power returns.

Key Takeaways from Chapter Three

- **Shyness is not your personality.** It's a learned response. Your nervous system's way of protecting you from perceived social threats.
- **Underneath shyness is fear.** Fear of being judged, misunderstood, or rejected. Often, it's rooted in past experiences that made visibility feel unsafe.
- **Shyness is a form of the freeze response.** When you feel exposed, your body stills, your mind blanks, and you shut down. It's how your system tries to keep you safe.
- **There are different types of shyness.** Situational, public, and chronic shyness all show up in different ways. None of them define you, unless you allow them too.
- **Avoidance reinforces the pattern.** The more you avoid, the stronger the association between being seen and being unsafe becomes. Awareness is the first step to unlearning.
- **There is nothing wrong with you.** You adapted to survive discomfort, but now it might be time to update those protective settings.
- **Your voice is not a threat. It's a gift.** You don't have to eliminate fear to move forward. You can begin by questioning whether fear is the truth.
- **Shyness is a learned response that can be unlearned.** With practice and self-compassion, you can shift the pattern and step into Quiet Confidence.

Chapter 4

Unlocking Quiet Confidence: The Shift That Changes Everything

"Either you decide to stay in the shallow end of the pool or you go out into the ocean."

— *Christopher Reeve*

The Confidence Myth

We grow up believing that confidence is something we either have or don't; that it's loud, effortless, and belongs to other people. The ones who speak first. The ones who shine in the spotlight. The ones who don't seem to hesitate before stepping forward. If you've struggled with shyness, you've probably convinced yourself that confidence is a distant dream; an elusive quality that some people are just born with. But what if I told you that real, deep, lasting confidence has been within you this entire time?

Not the forced, performative kind that drains your energy. Not the overcompensating, pretend-you're-not-shy kind. I'm talking about Quiet Confidence, the kind that allows you to move through the world with certainty, to trust yourself, and to take up space in a way that feels natural, not exhausting.

For years, I believed confidence was something other people had; people who were naturally charismatic, outspoken, and bold. I convinced myself that confidence looked a certain way, and because I didn't fit that mould, I must not have it. But confidence isn't something you either have or don't; it's something you uncover. It's already inside you, waiting to be recognised. And sometimes, it takes someone else to reflect that back to us before we can see it for ourselves.

The Power of Being Seen

Sometimes we need someone else to reflect back what we've been unable or unwilling to see in ourselves.

For years, I had this idea that I'd love to write a book. But every time the thought crossed my mind, I immediately shut it down. What have I really done that's worth writing about? Who would even want to read it?

I convinced myself that my life was too ordinary, too small, too unremarkable to be worthy of a book.

And then I met Jane.

Jane Turner is a writing coach and author who continues to support me today. From the moment we met, she saw right through me. When I first attended her workshop, I thought I was just there to learn about the mechanics of writing. But Jane had no intention of letting me hide behind technicalities or let me minimise what I had to say. She looked me straight in the eye and said, "Your story matters. Your experience matters. But there is no need to downplay it, because someone out there is waiting to hear it."

I wasn't ready for that. I wasn't ready to be seen like that. But something about the way she said it... calm, certain, without hesitation, stayed with me.

Jane introduced me to The Hero's Journey, the story structure found in almost every great narrative. The hero starts in their ordinary world, faces a challenge, and must leave their comfort zone. They struggle. They doubt. They fall. But then? They rise. They return home transformed, seeing everything, including themselves, differently.

As I listened, I felt something click into place. It wasn't just a story structure; it was my life.

My battle with shyness. My relentless struggle with self-doubt. My journey to finding Quiet Confidence. It wasn't just some personal struggle I had to get over; it was a story that could help others. And it was a story that I, for the first time, finally saw as worth telling.

Jane didn't just tell me I had confidence. She showed me by refusing to let me pretend I didn't. She was my mentor, my guide, the person who held up a mirror and said, "You've been capable this whole time."

And that's the thing about Quiet Confidence. It often starts with someone else believing in you before you're ready to believe in yourself. But what happens when you don't have that person yet? What if, for most of your life, the reflection you saw told a different story? That's where reframing comes in.

Reframing the Past: The Evidence You Missed

When you struggle with shyness, your brain becomes an expert at collecting evidence to support it. Every awkward moment. Every time you hesitated. Every instance where you felt different. It all gets stored away as proof.

Proof that you're shy, that you don't belong, that confidence is for other people. But here's the thing about our minds: they only see what they're looking for.

While I was busy gathering all the reasons I wasn't confident, I completely ignored the evidence that suggested otherwise.

The moments when I was lost in creativity, drawing for hours, completely uninhibited. The way my art teacher encouraged me, praised my talent, yet I brushed it aside because I didn't believe it mattered. The times I felt completely at ease, fully engaged, comfortable in my own skin. But I never counted those because I had already decided that I was shy.

I wasn't looking for confidence, so I never saw it. And if that's true for me, then it's probably true for you.

Think back to your childhood. Were there moments when you were completely at ease? When you didn't question yourself?

When you felt absorbed in something you loved, unbothered by how others saw you?

Confidence isn't just about social situations. It's about trusting yourself. It's about the moments when you feel safe to be exactly who you are. And I guarantee you've had those moments. You just didn't realise they were confidence in disguise.

Confidence Isn't What You Think It Is

Most people misunderstand confidence. They picture someone outgoing, fearless, and unwavering. Someone who never doubts themselves. But that isn't confidence. That's a performance, and performances don't last.

Confidence is something quieter. It's self-trust. The steady knowing that you can meet discomfort, face uncertainty, and still stay true to yourself. Real confidence doesn't mean being free from doubt. It means choosing how you respond, with calm, with presence, with clarity.

You are not a machine. You are not artificial. You are human. Even the most powerful among us feel fear and uncertainty. The difference lies in how they meet those moments, not with perfection, but with practice.

Quiet Confidence isn't about forcing yourself to be extroverted. It's about honouring your natural strengths. It's the ability to walk into a room and not shrink. To speak when you have something to say, not to impress, but because you trust your voice. To know that your presence is enough, even if you say nothing at all.

For years, I thought my quietness was the problem. But quietness was never the issue. The real issue was how I framed it. When I began to see my quiet nature as a strength instead of a flaw, everything shifted.

The Confidence You've Been Waiting For

Here's an important distinction: this isn't about becoming confident. It's about remembering that you already are.

You've already experienced confidence in your life. It just didn't look like what you expected. You've already had moments of self-trust, of ease, of feeling at home in yourself. And those moments? That's your true nature.

Your shyness, your doubts, your past; none of that has to define you anymore. What defines you is what you choose to focus on. And if you choose to focus on Quiet Confidence, if you choose to see yourself through a new lens, everything changes.

So here's your challenge: stop looking for confidence outside of yourself. Stop waiting for the perfect moment. Stop chasing an ideal that doesn't exist. Stop believing that confidence is something you earn rather than something you own.

Because the moment you drop the idea that you need to be someone else, you step into a confidence that's been there all along. Quietly, yet confidently, you step into who you were always meant to be.

Reclaiming Your Quiet Confidence

Before we move forward, I want you to pause. Because right now, at this very moment, you have an opportunity… a rare and powerful one. You get to rewrite the way you see yourself.

So, let's go back.

Close your eyes for a moment. Strip away the labels, the doubts, the insecurities. Strip away the voice that tells you you're not enough. Imagine that version of you who felt safe in your own skin; curious and unfiltered. Free to explore without fear. Before doubt crept in. Before shyness took hold. Before you learned to hold yourself back. That child, you, is still there. And they are waiting for you to remember.

I see myself as a kid, completely lost in my own world. A world where anything was possible. Where I could build, create, and dream without limits. I was obsessed with technology, always trying to figure things out. I loved sketching, designing imaginary homes, mapping out the future in my mind before it arrived. My brain was constantly inventing. I had no doubt that I could do anything, be anything.

And I laughed. A lot. I would talk gibberish with my family, saying the most ridiculous things, feeling completely uninhibited. I didn't care if it made sense. I didn't care if I sounded silly. I was just me, and it felt effortless.

And then there was the clay. I remember sinking my hands into it, feeling the cool, soft texture between my fingers. I wasn't thinking about what I was making, just creating. Moulding, shaping, letting my imagination guide me. It was messy. It wasn't perfect. But it didn't have to be.

For hours, I would lose myself in the process. No hesitation. No second-guessing. Just pure, uninterrupted flow, where mistakes weren't mistakes, just part of creating something new.

That was confidence. Not standing on a stage. Not being the loudest in the room. But being completely absorbed in something I loved, without fear, without needing permission.

So when did that change?

At some point, I started paying attention to what the world expected of me. I started editing myself. I abandoned parts of myself in an effort to belong. The wild, boundaryless creativity. The part of me that was totally carefree, limitless, and alive.

I started noticing where I was different, instead of where I was thriving. I focused on what made me feel awkward, instead of what made me feel free. I let doubt creep in and take over, and I stopped seeing the moments when I already had confidence.

Looking back, I realise confidence was never the problem. It lived in the laughter, in the imagination, in the moments I completely trusted myself when I was lost in creativity. And it's still there. Buried under years of self-doubt, sure, but not gone. Never gone.

Now, it's your turn.

I want you to sit with these prompts over the next page and respond to them not just with your mind, but with your heart:

- Remind me of one of my most precious memories.
- Show me what I most loved and treasured.
- Tell me what my greatest dreams were before the world told me what was realistic.
- Remind me who inspired me or influenced me the most. What about them captivated me?
- When did I feel most free? Most alive? What was I doing?
- What moments in my life made me feel seen? Truly seen?
- What part of myself have I abandoned in an effort to belong?
- What did confidence look like to me as a child, before I even knew what the word meant?
- What would it feel like to return to that version of myself? Not to go backwards, but to reconnect with the quiet confidence that was always there.

Here's the message I need you to hear:

You are not all shy. When you dig, and keep digging, you'll find that confidence is already inside you. You know it, you've felt it before. It is time to reclaim it.

Owning the Confidence That Was Always Yours

For too long, you've believed a story about yourself that isn't true. A story that told you confidence was something you

Quiet Confidence

lacked. That shyness was a limitation. That being quiet meant you were somehow less than.

But what if you let that story go? What if, instead of chasing confidence, you decided to see yourself differently—not as needing to be fixed, but as someone who was never broken to begin with?

Confidence has never been the absence of fear. It's never been about volume or dominance or trying to be someone you're not. Confidence is simply self-trust. And self-trust isn't something you earn. It's something you claim. Right now, in this moment, you have a choice. You can keep believing the outdated story that tells you you're not enough. Or you can choose to step into Quiet Confidence; fully embracing the person you already are.

Not everyone will understand this kind of confidence. That's okay; it isn't for them, it's for you. And when you claim it, quietly, yet confidently, the world will have no choice but to notice.

Key Takeaways from Chapter Four

- **Confidence isn't something you have or don't.** It's something you uncover. It already lives within you, even if it's been buried beneath doubt.
- **Shyness is not your identity.** It's a learned pattern of protection, not a permanent part of who you are.
- **Quiet Confidence is powerful.** Real confidence doesn't need to be loud. It lives in calm self-trust, not performance.
- **You've felt confidence before.** Moments of flow, play, creativity and ease are all proof. You just didn't recognise them as confidence.
- **The world's version of confidence is limited.** It often rewards extroversion, but there's strength in quiet presence too.
- **Your past holds evidence of strength.** When you reframe your story, you'll see that self-doubt wasn't the whole picture.
- **Belief often begins with being seen.** Sometimes it takes someone else reflecting your worth before you believe it yourself.
- **Self-trust is real confidence.** It means choosing to move forward with presence, even when fear is part of the journey.
- **You can choose a new story.** The old one kept you safe, but the new one will set you free.

Chapter 5

Flip the Switch: From Overthinking to Action

"Overthinking ruins you. Ruins the situation, twists things around, makes you worry, and just makes everything much worse than it actually is."

— *Karen Salmansohn*

Facing the Camera: The Moment My Mind Shut Down

3, 2, 1... Record. And nothing. Just a barely coherent sentence and a thousand outtakes.

Ever had to speak to the camera? The problem is, you're not speaking to a person, you're speaking to a lens. And it's awkward. You stumble, you freeze, and worst of all, it's all recorded... ready for playback, ready for judgement. Or at least, that's what I thought.

What makes this moment so disorienting isn't the act of speaking. It's the uncertainty, you don't know how it's going to be received. So your brain, doing what it does best, tries to fill in the gaps. And often, it fills them with worst-case scenarios. *What if I mess up? What if I look stupid? What if they judge me?*

The result: avoidance. Something I was very good at. I'd been rehearsing it for years.

The Camera Was My Shield

Looking back, my tendency to hide didn't start with adult responsibilities or professional pressure. It started long before that, with a childhood obsession.

I was the kid who loved technology. Give me anything with buttons, screens, or cables, and I was happy for hours. But nothing captivated me quite like the family video camera. There was something magical about being able to capture a moment and rewind time.

I filmed everything: family barbecues, birthday cakes, my siblings running around the backyard. But I was never in the footage, and that wasn't by accident.

I was always behind the camera. Always observing. Always directing, never starring. Because from behind the lens, I didn't have to perform. I didn't have to risk being seen, judged, or misunderstood. I could be part of the moment without being in the spotlight. And in the rare moments I ended up in front of the lens, I'd instinctively try to hide. I'd tilt my head, cover my face, or laugh it off. Anything to avoid truly being seen.

At the time, it felt creative. It felt safe. But what I didn't realise was that I was rehearsing a pattern that would follow me for years: stay behind the scenes, stay in control, stay unseen. What began as play became protection.

The Hidden Cost of Hiding

When you pay attention to that part of you that doubts, hiding can feel like the safest option. But it often comes at a cost. You stay quiet when you want to speak. You hold back ideas that matter. You skip the chance to press record, raise your hand, or step forward. You let the moment pass and convince yourself it wasn't the right time, or that you just weren't ready. But more often than not, what we call *not ready* is really this: *I don't believe in myself yet.*

Self-doubt tricks you into thinking you need to be flawless before you can be visible, but it's not perfection that builds confidence; it's practice, courage, and reflection. If you take every failed attempt personally, you miss the gift of growth. When you're learning a new skill like public speaking, being on camera, or stepping up in a meeting, it's normal to feel unsure. The problem is when you turn *I haven't mastered this yet* into *I'm hopeless.*

You weren't born walking, speaking, or reading; you learned through repetition, mistakes, and support, and just because you haven't mastered something yet doesn't mean you're no good at it; it simply means you're still learning.

You can build confidence by separating *I don't know how yet* from *I'm not good enough*. The two aren't the same, and they never were. That voice of self-doubt might be loud, but you don't need to listen to it. You can choose a different voice, the one that reminds you that learning is allowed, and growth takes time.

Overthinking, Judgement, and the Paralysis of Uncertainty

Overthinking is not deep thinking. It's rumination. A mental spiral that loops in on itself, offering no insight, no clarity, no resolution. Deep thinking leads somewhere. It builds. It reveals. Overthinking just spins. It fills your head with what-ifs, imagined judgements, and worst-case scenarios, with no answers, only anxiety.

What if I mess up?

Everyone will notice.

You don't know what you're doing.

Before you even begin, you're frozen. Trapped in your own mind. There's no space to grow when fear takes up all the oxygen.

We like to tell ourselves we're being careful, weighing up our options. But what we're really doing is feeding the fear. Each time we avoid taking action, we teach our brain that the fear was right.

So how do you break free? You ask yourself one simple question: Are my thoughts looping, or are they progressing?

If they're looping, pause and breathe. Bring your attention back to your body. The way forward is rarely found in the spin; it's found in the stillness that follows.

If they're progressing, that's a good sign. It means you're gaining insight or clarity. But even then, once the message has landed, you don't need to keep replaying it. Let it move through you, then move on.

The Brain Bank: How Fear Grows Through Repetition

Think of your mind like a bank. Every thought is either a deposit or a withdrawal. A moment of self-belief? That's a deposit. A moment of doubt? That's a withdrawal. If your account is filled with recycled thoughts like *I can't, I'm not ready*, or *I'll mess this up*, your confidence balance slowly drains away.

Studies suggest we have tens of thousands of thoughts each day. But most of them? They're repeats. We don't think new thoughts; we rethink old ones. And when those thoughts are rooted in fear, self-judgement, or inadequacy, we keep reinforcing the same unhelpful beliefs... over and over again.

In doing so, you've trained your brain to expect the worst, to anticipate failure, to shrink before you've even begun. Thought by thought, the narrative deepens. Eventually, the balance hits zero. Or worse, the account goes into overdraft. You feel stuck. Unsure. Numb.

This is when avoidance takes over. You stop trying. You scroll. You over-plan. You tell yourself you're resting, but really, you're avoiding. The circuit is overloaded. The system shuts down.

The Safety Switch

Your brain is built to keep you safe. It's like a house wired with a safety switch. The moment something feels too risky, it trips the circuit. It shuts you down to prevent damage.

But the problem isn't that the switch exists, it has become over-sensitive.

Now, any sign of discomfort, like speaking up, trying something new, or being seen, feels dangerous. The nervous system reacts the same way it would to real danger.

In those moments of hesitation, it's as if the lights go out. What could have been a moment of growth is suddenly misread by your nervous system as a threat. Instead of moving forward, you stay quiet, delay the decision, or distract yourself from the discomfort.

Your brain, doing its best to keep you safe, interprets the unknown as danger, even when it isn't. But you can choose to train your brain to see things differently, to reset your perception of risk and recognise that uncertainty doesn't always mean danger.

Outgrowing the Alarm

Confidence isn't built by pushing through terror. It's built by challenging what your brain believes is dangerous.

When you treat discomfort like danger, every step forward feels like a leap off a cliff. But discomfort is not the same as harm. Visibility is not the same as threat. Rejection is not the same as failure.

You've faced discomfort before. You've survived awkward moments. You've said the wrong thing, tripped over your words, felt exposed, and you're still here.

The real question is not *What if I fail?* but *What am I missing by not even trying?*

Reflection: Recalibrating Risk

Take a breath. Let yourself sit with these questions, gently and honestly:

- What exactly am I afraid will happen if I speak, act, or show up right now?
- How likely is that outcome? And if it did happen, could I handle it?
- When have I been uncomfortable before and come through stronger?
- What do I lose by staying silent or hidden in this moment?

- What's the cost of inaction, not just today, but over time?
- Could I be confusing discomfort with danger?
- If a friend were in my position, how would I encourage them?
- What's one small step I can take, even if I feel nervous?

Confidence doesn't begin with certainty; it begins with a willingness to learn, a willingness to risk imperfection, a willingness to show up even when the outcome is unclear. You won't always feel ready, and that's okay. What matters is that you're practising a new way of being, one quiet, courageous step at a time. With each step, you're teaching your nervous system something powerful: I can do this. I am safe here. I don't have to disappear.

Key Takeaways from Chapter Five

- **Overthinking can disguise itself as preparation.** What feels like caution is often avoidance. When you loop through thoughts without moving forward, you lose the chance to learn and grow. Clarity comes from action, not perfection.
- **Shyness often stems from a misreading of risk.** Your brain has learned to associate discomfort with danger. But discomfort isn't a threat, it's often the space where growth quietly begins.
- **Self-doubt keeps you hiding behind the lens.** Avoidance may feel safe, but it also keeps you invisible. Reclaiming confidence begins with stepping into the frame, even when it feels awkward.
- **Confidence is a learned skill.** You don't have to be born ready, just willing to practice being seen.
- **There's a difference between *I'm still learning* and *I'm not good enough*.** Mistaking inexperience for inadequacy blocks growth. You build confidence when you reframe failure as feedback.
- **Progress starts with one small step.** You don't need to eliminate fear to move forward. Even a tiny action can interrupt the cycle and begin to rewire your nervous system.
- **You are more capable than your fear suggests.** There's proof in your past that you've faced hard things and made it through. Let that truth guide you more than the uncertainty does.

Chapter 6

The Confidence Trap: Breaking Free from False Security

"We are so scared of being judged that we look for every excuse to procrastinate."

— *Erica Jong*

The Illusion of Confidence

Have you ever convinced yourself you were making progress, only to realise you were just circling the same safe spot? Maybe it looked like self-care. Maybe it felt like a smart delay. But beneath the surface, something didn't sit right. That's because what we often call confidence isn't confidence at all. It's comfort dressed up as courage. It feels protective in the moment, but it can keep us small.

This chapter is about recognising that trap, about seeing the difference between false confidence and the real thing. Building on what you've already learned about confidence, we'll go deeper. Because once you know how to spot the difference, you can begin choosing the kind of confidence that truly changes your life.

The False Confidence Fix

For years, I thought I'd found the key to confidence. I had discovered a magic elixir that could make me talk to people, say things without overthinking, and even take up space in a way I never had before: alcohol.

The first time I drank at a party, I wasn't the quiet guy in the corner anymore. I wasn't over-analysing what to say or second-guessing every facial expression. I was relaxed, talkative, and free. For the first time in my life, I thought, *so this is what confidence feels like*. But it wasn't real. It was borrowed. A trick that only worked until the effects wore off. The next morning, I was right back where I started, only now with the bonus of regret and a headache.

Still, I kept doing it. Because even though I knew deep down it wasn't a true fix, it was easier than doing the real work.

False confidence doesn't just show up in alcohol. It shows up in any behaviour that gives us a temporary sense of security without actually helping us grow. Including avoiding social situations because *I just prefer my own company*. Over-preparing for every little thing so you never feel caught off guard. Waiting for the right moment that never actually comes. Telling yourself, *I'm fine as I am*, while secretly wanting more.

False confidence feels good in the moment, but it keeps us stuck. It keeps us small. And at some point, we have to ask ourselves: Am I really confident? Or am I just comfortable, and missing the opportunity for growth? Or have I just become skilled at avoiding discomfort?

Avoidance: The Other Confidence Trap

There's another kind of false security we don't talk about enough, the kind that disguises itself as self-care but is actually avoidance. I used to believe I was doing the right thing by protecting my energy.

I need time to recharge, I'd tell myself as I turned down another invite. *I'll start next week,* I'd say as I pushed my goals further down the road. And yes, introverts do need downtime. That part is real.

But sometimes, the line between healthy restoration and fear-driven avoidance gets blurred. And when that happens, we start convincing ourselves that staying comfortable is the same as staying safe, but it's not. Confidence isn't built in isolation. It's built in action. It's built in doing the thing before you feel ready, safely and with the right strategy.

The reality is, I wasn't recharging; I was hiding. I wasn't preserving my energy; I was avoiding situations that made me uncomfortable. I wasn't protecting myself; I was stalling my own growth.

The Moment It Clicked: The Permission Trap

I remember the exact moment I realised that playing it safe was holding me back from the life I wanted. I was sitting at my desk, staring at a half-finished project. It had been sitting there for months, untouched. I told myself I was *waiting for inspiration*, that I needed more time, that I wanted it to be perfect before I put it out into the world.

But the truth was that I was waiting for permission. Permission from whom? I don't even know. Maybe from some invisible authority figure in my head. Maybe from the world itself. Maybe from the future, hoping that one day I'd wake up magically fearless, ready, and certain. But that day never came. Instead, I sat there, frozen. Because the second I finished that project, it would be real. And if it was real, that meant people could judge it. Judge me.

And that's when it hit me: this is why I stay stuck. Not necessarily because I'm not talented enough or don't have good ideas or lack confidence, but maybe I don't let myself make decisions from that place of inner intuition. I was still waiting for the world to show me the next step. But the world doesn't work like that. Nobody is coming to give me permission. I had to give it to myself, and so do you.

Breaking Free from False Confidence

If you recognise yourself in this, it doesn't mean you've failed. It means you've been adapting, surviving, doing your best with the tools you had. And now, you're ready to choose something different.

Here's what matters: real confidence doesn't feel like a sudden high. It's not a rush of liquid courage or a performance fuelled by adrenaline, and it doesn't come from waiting until everything is perfect.

Real confidence is built when you prove to yourself, again and again, that you can handle discomfort with intention. With a plan and with compassion.

It comes from:

- Saying yes to something that stretches you without overwhelming you.
- Speaking up, even when your voice shakes; and knowing what you want to say.
- Showing up, even when you feel like hiding; and having tools that help you stay grounded.

You don't need to force yourself to leap into the deep end. But it helps to gently question whether you're still waiting for fear to leave before you move forward.

Because false confidence keeps you stuck. Real confidence moves you forward; deliberately, strategically, and quietly.

But What Does Real Confidence Actually Look Like?

Not the over-the-top, "look at me" kind of confidence. Not the forced kind that feels like an act. I'm talking about Quiet Confidence, the kind that doesn't need to be loud to be powerful.

It's the kind of confidence that doesn't wait for permission, the kind that knows you belong in any room you walk into, and that your voice matters, even if it's the softest one in the room. So let's take a moment to envision it. Not in some distant, wishful-thinking way, but in a way that feels real, tangible and possible.

Envisioning Your Quiet Confidence

Let's pause for a moment. You've spent years waiting, waiting to feel ready, waiting to be "good enough," waiting for confidence to magically appear. But what if, starting today, that waiting were over?

Imagine you wake up tomorrow morning, and something has shifted. The shyness, the overthinking, the hesitation; it's no longer running the show. You don't know exactly how it happened; maybe it built slowly, or perhaps it occurred in the quiet moments. But today, you move through the world with Quiet Confidence. What's different? Go deeper. Observe.

- How do you wake up? Is your first thought different? Do you feel lighter? More excited about the day ahead?

- What's your body language like? Do you carry yourself with ease? Do you walk with presence?
- What do you no longer overthink? Where has the hesitation gone?
- How do you handle challenges? If something unexpected happens today, how do you respond?
- How do you speak? Do you express your thoughts without second-guessing? What does it feel like to trust your own voice?
- Who do you connect with? How do your relationships shift when you show up differently?
- What have you stopped apologising for?
- Where do you feel the most like yourself?

Write it down. Don't just imagine it, let yourself feel it. Place yourself in that version of you and take a look around. This is how you bring your mind and body back into sync. Not in some distant future, but in the small, everyday moments where you choose to believe you already belong.

Key Takeaways from Chapter Six

- **False confidence can mimic progress.** Short-term fixes like overpreparing, hiding behind humour, or using alcohol may feel empowering in the moment, but they delay real growth.
- **What feels like self-care can sometimes be avoidance in disguise.** Time alone is necessary, but when comfort becomes a hiding place, it stops being restorative and starts reinforcing fear.
- **Waiting for permission is disempowering.** You don't need to wait to be ready or chosen. Confidence begins the moment you stop deferring your power and start showing up for yourself.
- **Real confidence is built through discomfort, not recklessness**. It grows from small, deliberate actions that stretch your comfort zone and remind you of your ability to meet the moment.
- **Quiet Confidence begins with self-trust.** Even when nerves arise, you can return to your centre and speak from a place of calm, without needing to prove or perform.
- **You already hold confidence within you.** You've felt it before, in creativity, connection, clarity. Reconnect with that version of yourself and let them guide your next steps.

Chapter 7

The Quiet Strength You Forgot You Had

"You are the author of your life. So please don't let anyone including yourself make you think otherwise. If you feel like you don't like how your story goes, just write it differently. You have the tools, the courage, the power...you have it all!"

— *Iva Kenaz*

The Stories We Tell Ourselves

Every belief you hold about yourself started as a story. Stories about who you are. Stories about what you're capable of. Stories about what you *can't* do. And the problem with these stories? They aren't always true.

Most of them weren't even written by you. They were written by the people around you; by a throwaway comment from a teacher, by an embarrassing childhood moment, by a situation that made you feel out of place. Over time, you took those moments and turned them into *facts* about yourself. But what if those stories were just interpretations? What if they weren't facts at all?

You don't have to keep living by a script you didn't write. You can change it. You can choose to tell a different story, one that aligns with who you truly are.

The Two Arrows: The Power of Interpretation

There's a Buddhist parable about two arrows. The first arrow represents the event; something happens to us: a mistake, a setback, or an embarrassment. It stings, but it's inevitable. Life is full of first arrows.

The second arrow, however, is our reaction. It's the meaning we assign to the event, the judgment we place on ourselves because of it, and the belief we carry away with us. And that second arrow? That's where we have control. We can't always stop the first arrow, but we *can* choose whether to keep wounding ourselves with the second one.

The Childhood Moment That Defined Me, Until It Didn't

I can still remember sitting in a classroom, feeling frozen. I was asked to speak, but my voice wouldn't come. My heart pounded, my palms went clammy, and every second stretched into what felt like an eternity.

The teacher's impatience. The awkward silence. The muffled giggles from classmates. That was the first arrow, a moment of pain I didn't choose. But almost instantly, I fired the second one.

I told myself:

I'm not good at speaking. I must be slow. I'm not as smart as everyone else.

Those weren't facts. They were interpretations manifested as stories my mind created in an effort to make sense of the sting. But they hurt more than the moment itself.

And every time my mind looped back to that memory, every time I replayed the scene, every time I rehearsed those same self-defeating thoughts, I was firing the second arrow again. Wounding myself with the past, long after the moment had passed.

I told myself that moment *proved* something about me. That it wasn't just a bad day, it was evidence. Evidence that I wasn't capable, that I wasn't quick enough, that I wasn't good enough.

I carried that belief for years. But then, years later, I learned something that shattered it. That same teacher, the one I had internalised as cold, dismissive, and impatient, had been battling a terminal illness. She was in the latter stages of cancer at the time.

And suddenly, the entire memory shifted. Her coldness wasn't about *me*. Her frustration wasn't proof of my failure. She wasn't dissapointed in *me*; she was dealing with her own unseen struggles. And even more telling? She treated *everyone* the same way. Nothing about her reaction had been personal. Nothing about that moment actually proved what I had told myself it did.

For years, I had let that memory shape my identity. I had used it as proof that I wasn't good enough, when in reality, it had *never* been about me in the first place. How many other moments in my life had I misinterpreted?

Noticing What You Didn't See Before

When I went back to that moment in the classroom, I started to notice things I hadn't seen before. I had always remembered the silence, the fear, the feeling of being frozen. But what about the moments before that?

I hadn't raised my hand; I rarely did. I was shy, cautious. But I was listening, I cared. I wanted to get it right. When the teacher called on me, I wasn't unprepared; I was afraid.

There was no real evidence that I was incapable. My teacher's impatience wasn't a reflection of my ability. My report card never once said, *Joel is a failure at speaking in class.*

In fact, in almost every other setting, I was a thinker. I was the kid who observed before jumping in, the one who carefully considered my words before speaking, the one who didn't rush to answer just to fill the silence.

That wasn't shyness; that was thoughtfulness. The same quality I once saw as a weakness, something that made me *less than*, was actually one of my greatest strengths. It had never been a story of failure. It had always been a story of deep thinking, observation, and quiet confidence waiting to be realised.

Your Story, Reclaimed

For too long, self-doubt has been the narrator of your story, and shyness its loyal companion. Self-doubt feeds the story that you're not ready, not worthy, not enough. And the shy response? It obeys. It urges you to shrink, to play it safe, to disappear just when you long to be seen. Together, they whisper, don't risk it, don't stand out, and whatever you do, don't speak up.

But what if you took the pen back?

What if, instead of letting self-doubt and the shy response shape your story, you allowed Quiet Confidence to take the lead, not with noise, but with calm, steady truth?

Your past doesn't define you; the meaning you give it does. And that meaning is yours to choose.

So let me ask you gently:

- What stories have you been carrying that were never true?
- Where have you mistaken someone else's reaction as proof of your inadequacy?
- Where have you assigned meaning to something that was never really about you?

As we embark on this inner journey, we acknowledge the power and the gift of story. The power to choose a different story. From this day forward, you can choose a different outcome, like a choose-your-own-adventure book! Not only that, you're going to go back and change the meaning behind the stories that left you with scars.

Your story isn't finished; it's just getting started. And you are the one who gets to write the next chapter. Before you realise it, you will become aware that your Quiet Confidence will become so familiar to you that you'll realise you've had it from day one.

It will come to you easily, like a memory that you hadn't visited for years. In fact, this is the beginning of discovering that you've had Quiet Confidence from the beginning. It's a journey of inner discovery, uncovering the pure essence of who you are.

In previous chapters, we've spoken about those childhood moments that planted the seeds of shyness and self-doubt within us. Over time, they hardened into an identity we thought we couldn't shake. But now, it's time to shake it loose.

At first glance, you might see your life as a series of events and circumstances that have happened to you. But what if there's something deeper at play? I invite you to consider that our lives are shaped not just by what happens, but by how we react. The second arrow. What we see and perceive is often just an echo of something deeper. An echo of belief, emotion, and meaning. Our reality is not built from events alone; it's built from the stories we tell ourselves about them.

You can learn to change the emotional weight those stories carry. To loosen the grip of old meaning and choose something kinder. That's the work I do with my clients every day, helping them rewrite what once felt fixed.

Who's the Author?

If your life were a story, who would be holding the pen? It's a question that puzzled me for years. I often wondered whether I was the author of my life or just an actor reading someone else's script. Was I living out my own story, or simply playing the role others expected of me? Was I in charge of what came next, or just trying to survive the lines and scenes handed to me?

Think of it like this: inside your mind, there are two authors. Two voices vying for control of your story. One of them is loud, anxious, and relentless. This voice is fear disguised as reason. It edits you before you even speak. It erases bold ideas before they make it to the page. This is the voice of self-doubt, the inner critic who plays it safe by making you small.

But the other voice? That's your Quiet Confidence. It's steady. It's clear. It's the voice that knows who you really are beneath the noise. It speaks not with force but with truth. And when you let it write your story, everything changes.

But here's the challenge: most of us have been letting the fearful voice hold the pen for far too long. We've let shyness write chapter after chapter until we started to believe that's just who we are.

We're going to change that. Right here, right now. Let's start with something simple, but powerful. Get yourself a journal. Choose one that feels good to touch. Make it yours. Buy pens and highlighters in colours that light you up. They're not just for decoration, they're tools for emotional clarity.

If you'd like some guidance with this process, I've created a companion workbook specifically designed to help you explore these emotions, thoughts, and turning points. Inside, you'll find reflective prompts and space to write freely to help you track your emotional landscape over time. You can find more details about the Quiet Confidence Workbook at Resources section nearing the end of this book.

To help you connect more deeply with your thoughts and emotions and begin shifting them, here are a few powerful journaling prompts to explore. Each question is an entry point, inviting you to get honest, stay curious, and reconnect with your inner world.

Start With Presence

Start by checking in with where you are right now, before the story, before the judgement.

- What am I feeling right now?
- Where do I feel it in my body?
- Was there a thought that triggered this feeling, or did the feeling appear before I noticed any thoughts?
- How can I stay with this feeling, just for a moment, without needing to fix it?

Naming the Pattern

Notice what's familiar. Notice the loop your mind is running.

- What's the story I'm telling myself in this moment?
- Have I felt this way before? When?
- Is this response trying to protect me from something?
- How do I usually react when I feel this way, and is it helping me?
- How is this pattern trying to keep me safe?

Reclaiming the Pen

This is where you interrupt the loop. This is where you begin to write a new response.

- What would Quiet Confidence say right now?
- If I weren't afraid of being judged, what would I do?
- How would I show up today if I believed I was already enough?
- How could I respond differently next time, even just a little?
- How can I support myself through this moment instead of avoiding it?

Letting Go

This is where you gently loosen your grip on what no longer belongs to you.

- What thoughts or labels no longer serve me?
- What am I ready to release today?
- What part of my old story am I rewriting?
- How do I know when a belief is ready to be let go?
- How can I challenge the story with self-compassion instead of shame?

Affirm the Shift

End by anchoring into strength. You've already survived so much. Remind yourself.

- What do I know to be true about who I really am?
- What strengths have helped me come this far?
- What small act of courage can I take today?
- How do I want to show up for myself right now?
- How can I practice Quiet Confidence in one small way today?

Every day, carve out a few quiet moments to write. You might choose a few questions from above, or you might feel like starting somewhere else entirely.

If the structured prompts feel too rigid today, try this instead:

Ask yourself, *How am I feeling today?*

Then let the words come: No judgment, no censors and no inner editor. Let it be raw, messy, and honest. This is your truth: not the version you perform, but the version that's been quietly waiting to be heard.

When you're done, revisit your words. Highlight the phrases that hold emotional charge. Use colour to identify what's rising: anger, sadness, fear, hope, joy, confusion. Over time, you'll begin to see the patterns. You'll notice which thoughts take up the most space. You'll begin to understand how your body and mind have been trying to protect you.

You'll begin to spot the second arrow, not just the event but the meaning you gave it. And from there, you can begin to change it. This is you stepping up and taking the pen back.

Rewriting Old Chapters

There's a quiet power in recognising that your story can change. As we've explored in earlier chapters, the shyness response that once felt like your identity? It was never the full truth. It was a pattern: learned, rehearsed, and reinforced until it felt permanent. But patterns can shift. Stories can be rewritten. And you're not who you were when that story first took hold.

Throughout this book, I've described shyness not as a flaw or fixed trait, but as a survival strategy. One that tried to protect you from discomfort, uncertainty, or judgment. Recognising it for what it is, that it was your nervous system's way of keeping you safe, isn't just a mindset shift. It's liberation.

Because once you see it as a response, not an identity, it loses its grip. You can study it, understand it and then choose a new response. The old story becomes something you can grow beyond, like a costume you no longer need to wear.

Shyness once ruled me. It whispered my lines before I ever spoke. It dictated what I could do, who I could be, how much I could ask for. But over time, I realised it wasn't a life sentence. It was just a series of old thoughts, replayed and recycled until they hardened into belief. But it was never gospel. And it can be unwritten.

In the words of the singer-songwriter Natasha Bedingfield -

> *"I am unwritten, can't read my mind, I'm undefined. I'm just beginning, the pen's in my hand, ending unplanned."*

Those lyrics became a declaration for me. A reminder that the pen was, and always had been, mine.

From This Day Forward

You can learn to start again. You can stop letting old stories define you. You can choose a new narrator; one who speaks from self-trust, not self-doubt. One who sees your silence not as weakness, but as wisdom. One who knows that confidence doesn't always roar. Sometimes, it's quiet. Sometimes, it simply says: *I'm here.*

At the very moment you feel shyness rising, try this: pause. Breathe. Notice it, not as a flaw, but as a signal. A familiar pattern showing up to protect you from uncertainty. Now, before you "show up anyway," there's something even more important: remind yourself that you're safe.

Ground yourself first. Feel your feet on the floor. Drop your shoulders. Slow your breath and speak gently to yourself: *I'm okay. This feeling will pass. I can handle this.*

Because real confidence doesn't ask you to perform through panic. It invites you to step forward from a place of stability. And then, when the ground beneath you feels just steady enough, picture yourself taking the pen back.

Acknowledge the old pattern for what it is, an echo of something that once tried to protect you. There is no need to resist it. Simply notice it, offer your gratitude, and with quiet intention, choose a new way forward. Speak when your voice feels true. Move when your steps feel steady and aligned. Show up not to prove your worth, but to honour what truly matters to you, the quiet truth that lives within your heart.

At first, it may still feel unfamiliar. You might tremble and overthink, that's okay. New chapters are always a little shaky. But each time you return to safety *and then* move forward, you strengthen a new pathway. You train your body to trust again. You reclaim a little more of your voice. And eventually, people will begin to see you differently. What they see is not necessarily another person; they will see another layer of you. And even more importantly, you begin to see *yourself* differently.

You'll realise that Quiet Confidence was never something you had to earn. It was always there, waiting patiently underneath the noise. Waiting for the moment you stopped needing to act. Waiting for the day you stopped waiting.

Quiet Confidence

You can let go of the need to be louder to be heard or the desire to be perfect in order to be powerful. You can show up as *you*, fully, freely, and without apology. There was never anything wrong with your voice, and I just wonder, maybe it's ready to be heard.

Key Takeaways from Chapter Seven

- **Every belief begins as a story.** Most of the stories we believe about ourselves were shaped by others, but that doesn't make them true. With awareness and compassion, you have the power to rewrite them.
- **Interpretation shapes your reality.** Life will always bring arrows. But it's the second one, the meaning you assign, that you get to choose. Change the story and you change the outcome.
- **Quiet Confidence begins with authorship.** Fear doesn't need to lead the way. When you take back the pen, you reclaim your power to shape your story.
- **Journaling is a tool for transformation.** Reflective writing isn't just venting; it's how you spot patterns, process emotion, and anchor new truths. It helps you cut through the noise and find your true voice.
- **Safety comes before visibility.** You don't have to push through anxiety. Build inner safety first, then choose small, aligned steps. That's how real confidence is formed.
- **You've always had Quiet Confidence.** It's not something to earn. It's something to remember. A part of you has always known the way, patiently waiting for you to trust it.

Chapter 8

The Moment You Stop Waiting

"It is in your moments of decision that your destiny is shaped."

— *Tony Robbins*

When the Waiting Ends

There comes a moment, not loud or dramatic, but quiet and undeniable, when something in you shifts. You realise you've been waiting: for the right time, to feel ready, or even for more confidence. You've been waiting for someone else to tell you it's okay to begin. Just like in school, when you raised your hand and waited for permission to speak, to ask a question, to go to the bathroom—always compliant, polite, and considerate. But then something changed.

You grew up, and suddenly, no one was giving permission anymore. Life asked you to decide. And sometimes, you did, beautifully. Intuition kicked in, and the next step felt clear. You flowed. But other times? Too much uncertainty. Too many options. Too much newness. And just like that, you were that kid again. Waiting, frozen, unsure who was in charge.

What we call indecision is often just fear in disguise. Fear of getting it wrong. Fear of choosing something we can't undo. So we tell ourselves we're being careful. We tell ourselves it's wise to wait or retreat at all costs!

But underneath the hesitation is often a quiet hope; that someone else will decide for us, that clarity will arrive if we wait just a little longer. But what if it doesn't? What if the real turning point isn't certainty, but the choice to act anyway?

The Fear Response We Don't Talk About Enough

Let's be clear: avoiding something doesn't mean you're weak. It means your nervous system is doing its job. When you hesitate to speak, answer the phone, or try something unfamiliar, it's not just in your head. It's your entire body sensing a potential threat and stepping in to protect you. But protection repeated becomes a pattern. Over time, that pattern becomes the lens through which you view every opportunity, every decision, every chance to grow.

You don't just hesitate, you freeze. You don't just pause, you defer, and you wait, and wait, and wait.

Here's what many people mistake about confidence: confidence isn't born from the absence of fear. It's built on trust; trust that you can meet the moment in a way that honours both your growth and your nervous system. That's why the answer isn't to push yourself off a cliff and hope you fly. That's not courage; that's pushing yourself through a traumatic event when you're not ready for it.

Real growth begins with safety. It starts with gentleness. Often, it means choosing something just slightly outside the lines of your old story. That could be changing your environment, but sometimes, it's simply showing up differently in the same one. And often, the scariest shifts start with the smallest things.

When the Small Things Feel Huge

For years, I was terrified to answer the phone, and I also felt deep shame and wanted to hide the fact that I was anxious about something that felt normal for most people. The sound of it ringing would send my heart racing. Every time I saw an unknown number flash across the screen, a wave of panic hit me.

Who was on the other line? What would they ask? What if I didn't know what to say? What if I said the wrong thing and embarrassed myself? I hated the ambiguity of it. Not knowing what was coming. Not being able to prepare.

And making a call? Even worse. Picking up the phone and attempting to dial numbers felt like stepping onto a stage in front of an invisible audience. I couldn't see them, but I knew they were there; listening, waiting, judging. So I avoided it.

I let calls go to voicemail and delayed returning them. I convinced myself it wasn't that important, but secretly, I was afraid of the uncertainty. And every time I avoided it, I deepened the belief that I couldn't handle it; that I needed more time, more confidence, more certainty before I could act.

The problem with waiting for confidence is that it never arrives on its own. While you can learn to access a confident state in the moment, to activate a calm, grounded response when it matters, lasting confidence is something you build. It is created through action. Gentle, repeatable action. Each time you show up with presence, even in discomfort, you reinforce the truth that you can.

Eventually, I made a new choice. I started answering the calls. I made the ones I'd been avoiding. And slowly, the panic softened.

I wasn't fearless, but I had found a way forward. That way forward taught me something that changed everything:

Confidence isn't about knowing what's on the other side of the call. It's about picking up anyway. And maybe you're thinking, "It's just a phone call." But that's exactly the point – it's never *just* a phone call. Because if fear can stop you from doing something so small, where else is it keeping you stuck?

You've Been Here Before

Maybe for you, it's not phone calls. Perhaps it's speaking up in a meeting or starting a conversation with someone new. Maybe it's putting your creative work into the world. The details don't matter. What matters is that moment of hesitation when your mind starts running through all the ways it could go wrong, all the ways you might fail, and all the reasons why you should wait just a little longer.

It's easy to think that hesitation means you're *not ready*. But what if hesitation was just part of the process? What if confidence isn't about eliminating doubt, but moving *with* it? What if all this time, you weren't stuck; you were just standing at the edge of the call, waiting to decide?

The Choice Is Yours

Every day, we're met with micro-moments of choice. Tiny openings where we can lean into discomfort and take action, or retreat into the safety of what's familiar. The more we retreat, the more we reinforce the belief that we can't. That we're not ready. That confidence is for other people, but not for us.

But every time we choose action, even if it's messy or imperfect, we prove to ourselves that we can. Confidence isn't something we're handed; it's something we build. Hesitation may show up, but it doesn't have to hold us back. It can be the very moment that invites us to grow. And when we answer the call, even with shaky hands, we begin to set ourselves free.

Sometimes, that call doesn't look bold or dramatic. Sometimes, it's quiet. A moment of choosing something different. A small shift that interrupts the old pattern. A whisper that says, this way instead.

That's how I began to reconnect with a part of myself I had long forgotten: by choosing stillness over striving, nature over noise, being over performance.

The Whisper I Chose to Hear

When I asked myself where my Quiet Confidence truly began, it wasn't on a stage or in a breakthrough conversation. It was in nature, in the stillness it brings. In one quiet moment where I stopped running, both literally and metaphorically.

But before I could find stillness, I had to move. I needed to get out of my head, so I turned to my body. I went for a jog along the river, hoping the movement might quiet my mind. I wasn't expecting anything profound, but as I ran, something in me began to soften.

It was here that I was suddenly reminded of the child within, that version of me that was a curious child of nature. I was reminded of the moss that grew across the tree trunk spanning the distance of the creek bed. The sounds of the bush came back to me: the birds, crickets, and cicadas. I was taken back to a time when life was simple. I was reminded of the connection that I had back then, the connection I felt when I was in natural surrounds. The memories came flooding back. The child within sent me natural beauty to quiet my mind. I was left with pictures in my mind that made me smile.

In that moment, my feet told me to slow down. I felt a little guilty because I knew I needed the exercise, but I'd already stopped. I had this unexpected desire to tear off my shoes and sit down on the grass, despite it being a little damp. Part of me hesitated for a second. Then I decided that I simply didn't care. I glanced around me, basking in the natural beauty.

I painted a canvas with my eyes; each glance followed a particular natural rhythm, like a soft, subtle brushstroke. I untied my shoelaces and removed my shoes and socks, which exposed my feet to the natural plush rug of grass beneath me. I felt the nerve endings in my feet lighting up as each blade of grass tickled my soles.

As I sat in the wet grass, bare toes wiggling in the green, I realised that with little effort I was suddenly reconnected, both to the beauty around me and to myself. This is the best kind of wi-fi that I'd forgotten existed! But still I questioned myself: if I could feel this way after something so simple, why shouldn't I make this part of my daily ritual?

My call to freedom came when I realised that the discomfort I had been avoiding wasn't something to fear; it was a signal. A deep, inner pull back toward who I had always been beneath the layers of hesitation and doubt. Answering the call wasn't just about stepping forward; it was about waking up. It was about reconnecting with the part of me that had always been there, waiting. It was the moment I finally understood: change wasn't just possible; it was already happening.

When you start doing things that are truly in alignment with what your true self wants, what your soul wants, you flourish and life becomes a lot easier.

As I began reconnecting with myself and exploring what helped me feel most grounded, I kept returning to one powerful source: nature. Nature doesn't perform. It just *is*. It doesn't rush, and yet, it never stops growing. And that's what I was learning to do, too.

While writing this book, I began to notice how even a short walk outside shifted something in me. My thoughts slowed. My chest softened. The urgency that usually pressed in began to ease. I didn't need to journal or meditate or solve anything. Just stepping outside and breathing in the wind was enough, because without realising it, I was entering a meditative state.

Sometimes, all it took was placing a hand on a tree or watching light flicker through leaves. Sitting beside a plant. Letting my eyes rest on something living and green. And in those moments, it felt as if nature gave my nervous system permission to exhale.

I came to realise that being in nature wasn't just pleasant. It was *essential*. It anchored me. It pulled me out of my overthinking mind and back into my sensing body. But perhaps most importantly, it quieted the noise long enough for me to hear the voice I had been drowning out for years, my own. Nature invites reflection, yes, but it also invites honesty.

It allows you to reflect your inner world with gentle clarity. When you slow down enough to notice the tremble of a leaf or the stillness between the sound of the birds, something within you softens. That softening offers access back to your truest self.

So if you ever feel overwhelmed or disconnected, if the noise in your mind becomes too loud or the world too demanding, step outside. Find the tree, the sunlight, the breeze. Let them remind you of your own rhythm. Because confidence, like nature, doesn't need to shout to be strong. It grows quietly. It roots itself deep. It flourishes through patience and alignment.

That discomfort I had been avoiding, the tight chest, racing thoughts, endless search for certainty, wasn't the enemy. It was an invitation. A quiet nudge to stop striving and come home to myself. A whisper beneath the noise, reminding me to return.

And there was something I nearly missed: I could have overridden it. I could have put my shoes back on, drowned it out with a podcast, and kept running. I could have decided it wasn't convenient, that I didn't have time to feel. But something in me said: *Wait. Listen.* And this time, I did.

Because that's where Quiet Confidence begins. It lives in the silence, not the roar. It rises not when the world finally quiets, but when you choose to pause and truly listen. Beneath the noise, there is a truth that has always been there, ancient and familiar: You are already whole. You are already home. And the best part? You can choose to return, anytime.

Choosing Confidence as a Habit

Here's what I've learned: confidence isn't a flash of inspiration or a lucky break, it's a habit. A muscle built through repeated choices, not grand gestures, but small, deliberate ones. It's speaking up when silence feels safer. It's showing up when shrinking feels familiar. It's answering the call when every instinct tells you to let it ring.

And with every choice, it grows. Fear might still be there, but it no longer runs the show. You stop waiting for courage to find you. You begin shaping it, step by step, even if your hands tremble. In doing so, you start a new pattern. One built on trust, presence, and quiet strength. And patterns, repeated with care, build new habits. Habits that change how you show up, not just once, but every day.

In this moment, you get to choose. Will you stay in the old pattern? Or will you take the first step toward your own quiet return?

Key Takeaways from Chapter Eight

- **Hesitation isn't weakness.** It's a signal that your body has learned through past experiences. Noticing it without judgment is where change begins.
- **Avoidance can feel like the safer option.** But what looks like caution is sometimes just fear rehearsing its old routine. Growth begins when you gently disrupt that loop.
- **Confidence doesn't rush in.** It arrives quietly through repetition. Through the small decision to show up, to try, to listen to yourself even when you're unsure.
- **Nature is more than soothing.** It reconnects you with what's true beneath the noise. In stillness, your real voice returns.
- **You've already started.** Every time you paused, noticed, and chose to move forward, even in discomfort, you answered the call.

Chapter 9

Stop Pleasing. Start Belonging.

"What you seek is seeking you."

— *Rumi*

The Day the Fear Began

There's a story my mother once told me about her first day of school. She was five years old, lining up with a group of wide-eyed kids, chattering with excitement about the classroom behind the door. But before they even stepped inside, the teacher walked down the line and smacked each child on the leg. There was no warning, no explanation, just punishment for talking.

The message was clear: you will obey. You will not speak out of turn. You will not disrupt the order. That was the moment my mother learned that curiosity was dangerous.

Quiet Confidence

I remember being struck by how casual she was when she told me, as if it were just how things were back then. But something in me ached. That was a child punished before she even had a chance to get it wrong. I asked her how that day changed her. She said she became "Goodie Two-Shoes": polite, quiet, and well-mannered. She did what she was told. She learned to please. And in that moment, I saw it: the origin story of people-pleasing.

Because I had one too. Growing up, if I wasn't being called *shy*, I was being called *nice*. Too nice, actually. The kind of nice that doesn't cause trouble. That always says thank you. That smiles, even when something doesn't feel right.

The kind of nice that gets rewarded, but never really seen. Looking back, I can see that I wasn't born nice. I was born sensitive, observant, and curious. But like my mum, I picked up early that there was a right way to be. And it usually meant being agreeable, silent, and easy-going. But in those moments, you're not truly being rewarded; you're simply avoiding the trouble that comes with conflict.

I didn't learn in joy; I learned in fear: fear of being called out, fear of being wrong, fear of being judged in front of the whole class. So I kept quiet and I kept small, but people didn't see the fear. They just saw a "good kid." And so, the performance began.

People-Pleasing Is Not Your Nature; It's a Strategy

If you've spent your life trying to be liked, this next part might be your aha moment. You weren't being fake; you were surviving.

People-pleasing is not a flaw. It's a brilliant, adaptive strategy your nervous system created to keep you safe. Through lived experience, you realised that pleasing others reduced the chance of conflict, that saying yes kept things calm, and that being agreeable earned love, or at least prevented rejection.

But at what cost? You lost touch with what *you* wanted. What *you* needed. You stopped expressing your truth and started over-editing yourself for approval. And it worked, until it didn't. Exhaustion set in, and then you started resenting. The realisation finally hit you; you realised that even when everyone liked you, you didn't feel loved. Because you weren't being *you*. You were being who they needed you to be.

The Most Dangerous Question You Never Asked

People-pleasers often ask, *What do they want from me?*

But the question they rarely ask is, *What do I want for me?*

It sounds simple, but if you've spent your life contorting yourself to be palatable, that question can feel terrifying. Because to answer it truthfully, you would have to risk being seen. Not the polite or filtered version of you. But the whole, complicated, powerful, messy, raw, and incredibly real version you've kept hidden underneath.

Here's the thing: you don't owe anyone your silence. You don't owe them your approval, either. And you certainly don't owe your energy to anyone just because they expect it. Your energy is precious.

Pleasing Keeps You Safe, But Stuck

I used to avoid conflict like the plague. Whenever I found myself in the midst of it, I couldn't handle it. I dodged arguments to keep the peace. I stayed quiet at all costs to avoid confrontation.

But like many introverts, if we quietly ignore our emotions for too long, it's like inflating a balloon. It keeps filling, little by little. Eventually, it's going to burst. What once looked quiet and agreeable suddenly turns into overwhelm, or even anger—triggered by something seemingly small. But it's not about that moment. It's the balloon breaking.

Pleasing feels like control. Everything on the surface appears harmonious, like you're the glue holding it all together. But that's the trick. It's not harmony; it's suppression.

Because when you're constantly scanning for other people's reactions, you're never actually living for you. You're shape-shifting. You're anticipating. You're managing everyone else's comfort while sacrificing your own.

All the while, you're hoping someone will notice. That they'll appreciate how much you're doing. That they'll finally give you the love and safety you've been bending over backwards to earn. But they won't. Because they don't see the real you, and you can't be loved for who you are when you feel like you may as well be reading lines from a script.

From Pleasing to Belonging

Here's the twist: what you're really craving isn't to be liked; it's to belong. Being liked is conditional. It's performative. It requires constant upkeep. You read the room, soften your edges, and play the part. But belonging is different. Belonging is rooted in truth. It doesn't ask you to earn your place. It invites you to take up space as you are.

When you're trying to be liked, you become a chameleon. You change colours to blend in. You adapt to keep the peace, to avoid rejection, to stay safe. But after a while, you forget what your true colours even are.

You can't be everything to everyone. And the more you try, the further you drift from yourself.

When you belong, there's no need to perform. You speak your truth and trust that the right people will stay. They stay because they see you for who you are. So if you've been wondering why the compliments feel empty, why your friendships feel shallow, or why you still feel lonely even in a crowd, it may be that you've been seen for the version you perform, not the one you truly are.

Not Everyone Gets a Say

Not long ago, I received a comment on TikTok that mocked the way I looked on camera. It wasn't thoughtful. It wasn't helpful. It was a personal attack on my physical appearance, the kind that says more about the person writing it than the one it's aimed at.

And here's the thing: I didn't take it to heart. I'm not made of stone, but I've learned how to tell the difference between genuine feedback and someone else's projection. I get to choose what lands, and what doesn't.

Most people who post nasty comments online aren't offering insight; they're looking for a reaction. Trolls hide behind empty profiles and blank avatars. They don't know you. They don't see you. They're not trying to connect. They're throwing darts in the dark, hoping to hit something soft.

You don't have to hand them the target. When you speak up, share something real, or stand for something that matters, not everyone will like it. They're not supposed to. That's the cost of authenticity. But the payoff? Your self-worth no longer lives in the hands of strangers.

You get to become the gatekeeper of your attention, your energy, and your truth. Not everyone deserves access to your nervous system. Not everyone gets a say.

Discernment is the lesson here. Knowing that just because something is personal doesn't mean you have to take it personally. Think back to the second arrow. The pain isn't just in what's said; it's in what we believe about what's said. And we only take it personally when it touches something we already fear might be true.

But when you've done the work, when you've softened your self-judgement and come home to your worth, it doesn't land the same way. Trolls lose their power. Their words can echo, but they don't stick.

Let them scroll. Let them scoff. You've got better things to do than perform for people who are committed to misunderstanding you.

You're not here to win everyone over. You're here to live, create, connect, and lead from a place that's real.

And when you do that, you'll find your people. The ones who don't need you to shrink or edit yourself for approval. The ones who recognise something familiar in your truth and think, finally.

Your Real People Are Not Impressed; They're Moved

Your people aren't the ones clapping because you performed well. They're the ones who sit with you when you fall apart. The ones who challenge you without shaming you. The ones who love you not despite your edges, but because of them.

There is no need to water yourself down to keep them. In fact, the more you reveal, the deeper the connection grows. That's the paradox of true belonging. The more *you* you are, the more magnetic you become to the people who truly matter.

Show up as you are, and the right people will stay.

Finding Your People

Once you stop performing, something remarkable happens: you feel alone.

Not forever, but for a moment, the world feels quieter. It's as if the sound has been turned down on everything and everyone who used to distract you from yourself. You've stopped over-functioning, stopped over-giving, and stopped apologising for existing. In that stillness, you feel the ache of absence, the absence of true connection.

But don't panic. This isn't loneliness; it's clarity. It's the sound of you no longer begging for belonging in places that were never built to hold you.

Now that you've stopped twisting yourself into knots for people who never truly saw you, it's time to look for something real: your people. The ones who don't need you to shrink, who aren't intimidated when you speak your truth, and who feel like exhaling.

You might think, *But where do I find them?*

You begin by knowing who they are.

Start by Getting Clear

Your people are out there, often where you least expect, once you know what to look for. They might not look like who you expected. They might not share your hobbies, your job, your background. What they *do* share is your values, your energy, your frequency.

When you're around them, your nervous system relaxes. You laugh easier. You speak without rehearsing. You don't feel the need to "earn" your place. You just... belong. Take a moment right now. Picture someone you feel completely safe with.

What do they bring into your life? How do they respond to your vulnerability? Do they listen to understand, or just wait to speak? Now ask yourself: where might this kind of person spend time? Not where they *should* be, but where they're already quietly thriving.

Are they in creative communities? Support groups? Book clubs? Volunteer circles? Breathwork workshops? Coffee shops with notebooks open? There's no need to go treasure hunting; all you need to do is start showing up where authenticity lives.

Because here's the truth: when you start showing up as yourself, your people recognise you faster. They're not looking for the mask. They're waiting for the real you.

You Don't Need Everyone

This is a beautiful truth. It set me free, and maybe it will for you too.

Old people-pleasing habits will have you chasing a crowd, assembling an army of acquaintances just to feel accepted. Let's be honest, no part of you needs a tribe of hundreds. You'd barely keep up with them unless you could clone yourself. What you need, what your nervous system craves, is a few real ones. The kind of connections where depth replaces noise.

Most introverts already know this in their bones. The volume of surface-level chatter is exhausting. But give an introvert a safe space, surrounded by kindred spirits, and suddenly they come alive. The quiet one becomes the storyteller. The observer becomes the spark. That's what safety does; it lets you unfold.

Because one safe friendship can be more healing than a hundred shallow ones. One honest conversation can melt years of silence. You were never meant to be everything to everyone. It was never about being liked by the masses. What matters is being met, as you are, by the ones who truly see you. So when the fear kicks in and the old reflex to perform returns, remind yourself gently: I'm not here to please the crowd. I'm here to find the ones who feel like home. The ones who simply get me.

Let Belonging Start With You

Here's the sacred reversal: you find your people by being your own first.

When you stop turning away from yourself, when you stay even in the messy moments, something powerful begins to shift. The more you choose not to abandon yourself, the less others seem to drift away. It isn't magic; it's alignment. You are no longer signalling that it's okay to be dismissed. You are showing up fully, and others begin to mirror that.

When you honour your truth, softly and steadily, something beautiful happens. Others feel safe to honour theirs. You stop performing and start meeting. You stop managing impressions and start making connections. No one is asking for perfection. You can choose to be here, as you are. That is where the real meeting happens, in the spaces where masks fall away and someone else sees themselves in your truth and quietly says, "me too."

When you stand tall in your realness, others gather. Not to fix you, elevate you or diminish you, but to meet you, stand beside you and offer their own presence in return. It becomes a quiet exchange, a natural give and take, where showing up as you are is not only enough; it is everything.

The Birth of Real Belonging

There's no turning back. As loud as my fears were, something deeper had taken root. A quiet, unshakable knowing. I had made a commitment to myself: I was no longer going to let shyness run the show. Who am I not to rise? Who am I not to speak? I had spent so long trying to please everyone, but something had shifted. I was beginning to trust myself more than my fear. I was no longer willing to hide.

All those years ago, when I released the first edition of *Quiet Confidence*, this mission was still in its infancy. The message was just beginning to take shape. I was finding my voice as I wrote, letting the idea breathe, stretch, and grow into something real. And then I pressed the button. A quiet concept became a lived experience.

I didn't just start a Facebook group. I created a gathering. A space. A doorway into something shared. I planned our first face-to-face meetup in Sydney, unsure who would come, but certain it needed to exist. And then people showed up. Beautiful, brave humans I had never even met, willing to step into a room with strangers and speak from the heart; vulnerable and real.

What started as an idea became a community. A like-minded circle built not on small talk, but on something deeper. We weren't there to perform, we were there to connect. I remember the moment before it all began. The nerves whispering, *Who am I to lead this?* But something steadier rose within me and replied, *Who are you not to? You have lived this. You have walked it. Now invite others to walk with you.*

In the sessions that followed, we didn't just talk. We connected, shared, and sat together in stillness. In that silence, something golden emerged. It wasn't awkward or empty. It felt sacred, steady, and safe.

When we did speak, we spoke from the heart. There was no need to impress or pressure to perform; just the rare, healing permission to show up exactly as we were.

If I had ever needed proof that this path was the right one, I had found it. Not in applause, but in presence. In the soft unfolding of people returning to themselves, together. We didn't just build a group, we found belonging.

And yes, over time, and especially during COVID, some of that face-to-face connection faded. We tried to recreate it online, but something was missing. Because once you have tasted real connection, the curated kind no longer satisfies. But even in the quiet years, even when the community sat dormant, something inside me had changed.

Because once you realise you have been performing your whole life, and suddenly feel the freedom not to, you don't forget. You don't go back. You carry that awareness with you. It becomes your compass. That is what true community feels like. Not from a place where you finally feel enough, but a place where enoughness was never in question.

And whether or not you believe that like attracts like, here is what I know for sure: when you evolve, the people you draw in will reflect that evolution. As you rise, so will the company you keep.

Key Takeaways from Chapter Nine

- **People-pleasing is not your fault.** It began as a survival strategy, an adaptive response shaped by fear, not your true nature.
- **Niceness isn't the same as truth.** The performance of politeness often masks deep fear. What looks agreeable can be a learned way of staying safe.
- **You weren't born to be liked by everyone.** What you truly crave isn't approval; it's belonging. And belonging doesn't require performance.
- **You get to choose who gets a say.** Not all opinions deserve your energy. Discernment is your protection.
- **Trolls don't know you.** Criticism without connection is projection, not truth. Let them scroll.
- **You can't be everything to everyone.** The more you try, the more you drift from yourself.
- **True connection comes from truth.** One honest conversation can melt years of silence. You don't need a tribe of hundreds, just a few safe, real ones.
- **Belonging starts with you.** When you stop performing and choose to be fully yourself, others feel safe to do the same.

Chapter 10

The Secret Language of Confidence

"Your body is your subconscious mind."

— Candace Pert

When Your Body Feels Like the Enemy

You don't always notice the moment it begins. Sometimes it arrives as a whisper. A shallow breath. A tightening in your chest. A clench in your jaw you hadn't realised was there until it aches. Other times, it crashes in; loud and undeniable. A pounding in your chest so fierce you're convinced the whole room can hear it. A wave of heat rising up your neck. That sudden sense that something is wrong, even when nothing on the outside has changed.

I'll never forget the day of that job interview. I had done everything right. I looked sharp and rehearsed every possible answer, walked through every scenario in my head. My mind said I was ready. But the moment I sat down in that waiting room, my body told a different story. My heart thudded wildly, as if trying to escape my chest. My mouth dried out. My hands began to shake. My legs bounced with nervous energy I couldn't control. And in that moment, I wasn't just anxious. I was ashamed. Ashamed of what my body was revealing. Ashamed that I couldn't hide it. Ashamed that I couldn't hold myself together when it mattered most.

When they called my name, I stood, but I wasn't really there. I felt myself float out of my body, watching from somewhere far away. Already spiralling. Already assuming I had failed. I stumbled through the interview, forgetting names, forgetting answers, forgetting myself. I walked out feeling small, collapsed on my bed, and let the familiar voice of self-blame take over.

What is wrong with me? Why can't I be normal? Why does this keep happening?

Maybe you've been there too. In a meeting or on a date or even standing in line at the grocery store, suddenly forgetting why you came. Your mind knows you're safe, but your body disagrees. You try to smile. You try to breathe. You nod at the right moments, hoping no one can see the chaos happening inside. You look composed, but you're bracing; for failure, exposure or complete collapse.

And the cruelest part is, you start to believe it's your fault. You start to believe that if you were more confident, this wouldn't be happening. That if you were stronger, your body wouldn't fall apart like this. And slowly, quietly, you begin to see your own body as something to be managed. Something unreliable. Something working against you.

And somehow, your body becomes the enemy. But what if that story isn't true? What if your body isn't betraying you at all? What if it has been protecting you, in the only way it knows how? What if every tremble, every surge of heat, every pounding heartbeat is a signal, not of failure, but of survival? What if it's intelligence, not malfunction?

That racing heart is your body's way of delivering enough oxygen to keep you going. Those shaky hands are a result of adrenaline coursing through your system, seeking release. The tightness in your throat is the echo of a voice that was once silenced, now rising because something needs to be heard. Because you matter, and so does what you have to say.

What you thought made you different in all the wrong ways may actually be your greatest source of truth and depth. The body you've spent years trying to override may be wiser than you ever knew. The problem isn't your body. The problem is the meaning you've been taught to assign to it. The messages you inherited that told you to numb, suppress, override, and dismiss. The inner signals you were taught to fear or ignore.

And when you live disconnected from your own body's truth, you lose access to your deepest wisdom. You lose the signals that tell you when something is off, when something needs care, when something needs to change. You lose the very compass that was designed to guide you home.

So here's the shift. It's not about fixing your body. It's about learning to listen to it; gently, compassionately, and with curiosity. It's about transforming those once-terrifying signals into sacred communication. Letting your body speak, and choosing not to silence it.

Not *Get it together* or *Stop being like this.*

But:

I hear you, I'm with you, and you're safe now.

This is where change can begin—not in force, but in listening. Because when you stop fighting your body and start meeting it with presence, things begin to shift. Your breath deepens. Your mind softens. And the old story that framed your body as the enemy starts to loosen its grip. Not in one dramatic moment, but gradually, with each act of self-kindness. Breath by breath, you come home to yourself.

The Body Remembers What the Mind Tries to Forget

There are things you've survived that your mind no longer talks about. Perhaps it never really did. Maybe it boxed them up, wrapped them in silence, and tucked them away somewhere out of reach. You learned to keep going, to stay functional, to smile and push through. But your body? Your body never stopped listening.

Even when life looked fine from the outside. Even when there was no yelling, no visible harm, no bruises to explain the ache.

Your nervous system was paying attention. And so was your subconscious. That deeper, emotional part of you that speaks in sensation, not language. The part that stores everything you were too young, too overwhelmed, or too unsupported to process.

It remembered the weight in the air when someone's mood shifted. The sound of footsteps that made your stomach tighten. The silence that followed after you spoke up and were ignored. It remembered how you shrank when you sensed disappointment, how you braced for impact, not always physical but emotional. It remembered the moment you learned that being too much or not enough came with consequences.

These aren't just memories. They're imprints, etched into your nervous system in moments when you felt uncertain, unheld, or unsafe. Each time something similar happens, whether it's someone raising their voice, hearing a certain phrase, or sensing a shift in the energy of a room, your body reacts before your brain catches up. That's because the subconscious stores memory through sensation rather than words. It remembers through feeling.

You might not recall the details of every difficult moment, but your body does. It flinches, it tenses, it withdraws, all in the name of protection. These responses were never random. They were learned through repetition and reinforced by your environment, forming invisible links between emotions and experiences. That's what anchoring is.

An anchor can be formed in pain, in fear, in stress, but also in beauty, in joy, in moments that felt safe. Think about the last time you walked down the aisle at your local supermarket and heard a song that immediately transported you back to your childhood. That's an anchor. A moment in time emotionally imprinted and tied to a sound, a smell, a place, or even a conversation. Your body remembers what mattered, and it remembers how it felt.

So your body did what it was beautifully designed to do. It adapted. It tensed and braced, scanning for danger in every glance, every silence, every shift in tone. It learned to shut down, to freeze, to disappear when the world felt too scary to face. And in doing so, it began to create a map for survival, etched not in words but in reflexes: one shallow breath at a time, one flinch, one skipped heartbeat, one lingering moment of silence that whispered, stay small, stay safe.

But this wasn't just a physical reaction. It was your subconscious mind stepping in. The part of you that holds emotion, memory, belief, and instinct all at once. When something was too much for your conscious mind to make sense of, your subconscious took over. It decided what to store, how to respond, and most importantly, what it all meant.

Because meaning is powerful. When something hurts deeply enough, especially without comfort, it doesn't just stay as a memory. It becomes a message. A belief. This is who I am. This is how life works and how I see the world. This is what I must do to be safe. And when that message goes unchallenged, it weaves itself into your identity.

If no one ever explained what was happening, if no one told you it made perfect sense for your body to respond the way it did, you likely blamed yourself. You thought you were overreacting, too sensitive, too dramatic, or too shattered. But you were still whole underneath.

You were just overwhelmed. You were alone with something too big for your system to carry. And your body, loyal and wise, remembered. It remembered how to shut down and check out. How to armour itself against the next moment that might feel like danger. It did not forget, because forgetting would have made you vulnerable again.

The good news is, what's been learned can also be unlearned. The patterns you developed in survival were intelligent, necessary, and protective. But they are not fixed. The part of you that once braced for danger can also learn to soften. The same inner system that learned to anticipate threat is capable of learning what safety feels like too.

You may not have had the tools back then. You may not have had the language or the support, but you do now. Your body is listening. That deeper part of you, the part that's held so much for so long, is still open to learning something new. When you begin to respond to yourself with steadiness, patience and kindness, a quiet shift begins. Your nervous system notices. Little by little, it begins to loosen its grip.

This process isn't about striving for peace or pretending everything is fine. It's about allowing yourself to feel safe enough to be real. To offer what was missing the first time: spaciousness instead of pressure, tenderness instead of tension, and the quiet reassurance that you don't have to hold it all alone.

You cannot erase the past. But you can change the way it lives inside you. You can hold the younger parts of yourself with the compassion they never received. You can rewrite the meaning your subconscious once gave those memories.

They say the body keeps the score. And it does. But you are allowed to change the game. You are allowed to rewire your relationship with safety. You are allowed to live in a body that no longer flinches at joy. You are allowed to create a present that feels different from the past. This is the turning point. Not just in your thoughts, but in your nervous system.

I used to look at my past with shame, wishing I could rewrite the timeline and trade it for a more confident version of me. I wanted to forget it all. But moving on was never about sweeping the past under the rug. What I've come to realise is this: you can reach back and reconnect with the version of yourself that lived well before the fear ever existed.

You Don't Have to Deserve Calm to Access It

I'm going to make a bold statement. One that might surprise you, but also might land in a place you've always known deep down. Our brains have become addicted to drama.

We consume it constantly. We binge-watch series built around tension and betrayal. We scroll past thirty-second clips that jolt us with shock, rage, or heartbreak, then move on to the next. The algorithms are designed to hook us with chaos. And after a while, the nervous system begins to expect it. Crave it, even. We're so used to emotional whiplash that stillness can feel almost foreign. But life is not Netflix. And your nervous system is not a television set.

The reality is, stimulation is addictive. And if you've been raised in unpredictable environments or have spent years walking on eggshells, your body has learned to associate hyper-vigilance with safety. So when things go quiet, it doesn't feel peaceful. It feels suspicious. Like something bad must be coming. So you keep scanning and searching for the next thing to fix, the next fire to put out, the next drama to prove yourself in.

We can enjoy stories that move us. We can feel the thrill of a well-written plot twist. But real life, our everyday, moment-to-moment experience, isn't meant to be a constant adrenaline rush. When we live in that state for too long, we burn out. We lose ourselves trying to keep pace with something we were never designed to sustain.

And just because there's drama all around you, doesn't mean you have to participate in it. You don't need to subscribe to it, carry it, or take it on and call it yours. The world will always have noise, but your inner world can learn a different rhythm.

That is the distinction I want you to begin to feel. The world around you and the space within you are not the same thing. They don't have to mirror each other. Just because there is chaos out there doesn't mean there must be chaos in here.

But if you've spent your life on high alert, that might sound impossible. Like many of us, you might have been taught that calm was something you earned. That rest was a reward and ease had to be justified. You learned, often without words, that peace was for later. For when the work was done, the people were happy, the rules were followed, and your worth was proven beyond doubt.

So you kept going. You tried to be everything for everyone. You overthought every move, every word. You felt guilty for resting. You felt selfish for needing space. And maybe, even now, you still find yourself reaching for the next task, just to feel like you've earned your place in the world.

But what if calm isn't a destination? What if it isn't something you deserve or unlock or finally arrive at once you've crossed some invisible finish line?

What if calm is something you *remember*?

A natural state your body has known since the beginning, before the expectations, before the performance. It's a place your nervous system can return to simply because it belongs to you. You are allowed to breathe, even when the list is unfinished. You are allowed to rest, even without needing to explain why.

The first time I noticed this pattern in myself, it was subtle. My mind was racing, heart beating faster than the moment required. That familiar voice was creeping in; the one that tells me I need to fix something, control something, or prove something. But this time, I did something different. I paused. I placed a hand over my chest and said softly, *You're allowed to rest now.*

And something shifted. Not all at once, not in some magical wave of transformation. But just enough for my breath to come back and for my shoulders to lower. Enough to remember that I wasn't faulty; I had simply found myself caught in a loop I didn't yet know how to escape.

That's what nervous system healing is. It's not glamorous or loud. It's not some big, performative thing you show to the world. It's quiet, subtle, and sometimes invisible. But it's powerful. Because every time you choose to pause instead of push, you're teaching your body a new way to live. You're reminding yourself that calm doesn't have to be earned; it can be accessed whenever you choose.

If you're caught in that loop, if your body feels tight, if your thoughts are racing, if you're looking for the next drama to justify your aliveness, pause.

Place your hand over your chest and remind yourself, in your own words if you need to, that you don't have to stay in that state. You don't have to be at war with your own breath. You don't have to prove anything to deserve the quiet. Because the most radical thing you can do in a world addicted to drama is choose not to play along.

And the most healing thing you can offer your nervous system is permission to rest, simply because you exist. That alone is reason enough.

How I Learned to Reframe My Anxiety

I'll never forget the day of that radio interview. Bondi Beach. Blue skies. A warm Tuesday morning. It should've felt like a dream. And in some ways, it was. But inside me, a storm was brewing.

I'd been invited to speak live on *Bondi Radio* with Jane Turner. It was a surreal opportunity, and something a former version of me would have immediately run from. My head told me I'd be fine. I'd prepped. I knew my story. I believed in my message. But the moment I stepped into the studio, something shifted.

My heart started pounding. My mouth went dry. The familiar flutter in my stomach arrived. Not gentle like butterflies, but wild and chaotic, like they were staging a mutiny.

When Jane turned to me and asked, "How are you feeling?" a past version of me would've panicked. That question had always felt like a trap—like admitting any fear meant I wasn't ready. Like naming my nerves would make them worse.

But this time, something was different. I paused. I took a breath. And I said honestly:

"I'm excited… but there are a few butterflies."

She smiled and replied with something I'll never forget:

"It's all right to have butterflies in your stomach. Just get them to fly in formation."

In that moment, something clicked. My body wasn't betraying me; it was preparing me. Those flutters weren't signs of failure;

they were signals of something important. I was about to step into something meaningful. Of course, my body knew. It always knows.

And so, when we went live on air, I didn't try to suppress the butterflies. I didn't try to pretend I was fearless. I just let them fly, and they flew in formation.

To my own surprise, I didn't freeze or go blank either. I didn't run out of words, as I had always feared I would. I spoke with presence, clarity, and Quiet Confidence. When the hour was over, I didn't want to leave. I felt light, energised, and alive.

If I hadn't been in office clothes, I might have jumped straight into the ocean in celebration. It wasn't just about completing the interview; it was about embracing the butterflies. It was about giving myself a new story to live within—one where the physical sensations were not a threat, but an ally.

Because what I've learned is this: anxiety and excitement are chemically identical.

The body reacts the same way; it's our *interpretation* that changes everything. And that means you get to choose the meaning.

You get to think,

This flutter in my chest means I care.

This energy in my body means I'm awake to this moment.

This isn't fear; it's fuel.

That day, I didn't silence my body. I partnered with it. And in doing so, I gave myself back something I didn't even know I'd lost: the right to belong in my own skin even while shaking.

Listening to the Whisper Before It Becomes a Scream

Most of us weren't taught to listen to the body. We were taught to override it. To push through the discomfort. To ignore the tightness, the restlessness, the signals that whispered, *something isn't quite right*. And when pushing didn't work, we were taught to panic. To assume there must be something wrong with us. So we turned to Google, typed in our symptoms with trembling fingers, and braced for the worst. And sure enough, the results confirmed every fear we didn't know we had. Our minds spiralled. We fixated, obsessed, played detective with our own biology. But what we called a crisis was often just our nervous system asking for care.

Like we've touched on before, those early sensations, the flutters in your stomach, the tension in your jaw, the breath that catches before your thoughts do, aren't malfunctions. They're messengers. Not signs that something is wrong with you, but signals that something doesn't feel quite safe.

The body rarely starts with an outburst. It is not trying to overwhelm you. It starts quietly. A shift. A murmur. A subtle tightening in the chest. A dry mouth. The nervous swallow before a difficult conversation. These aren't random sensations. They are patterns. Early signals from your nervous system that something feels off, often long before your conscious mind understands why.

But if you've spent a lifetime brushing past these whispers, dismissing your instincts, numbing your discomfort, and powering through without pause, your body eventually stops whispering. It starts raising its voice. It begins protecting you in the only way it knows how: by shutting things down or setting alarms off. That is when the whispers turn into screams.

It looks like sudden panic. Like the floor falling out from under you. Like a brain that won't stop spiralling or a body that refuses to move. It feels like being hijacked from the inside. Not because you are weak, different or strange, but because your body has been trying to reach you for longer than you realise, and now it has no choice but to get loud.

That is what happened to me in that job interview all those years ago. I had prepared, polished, and practised. I walked in thinking I was ready. But the moment I sat down, my body erupted. My heart pounded. My breath tightened. My thoughts scrambled. I didn't know what was happening. I thought I was failing. I thought I was falling apart. But in hindsight, I wasn't failing at all. I had simply reached the volume my body needed to get my attention. All those whispers I had ignored for years had finally become too loud to suppress.

These days, I try to catch it earlier. I try to honour the whisper before it turns into a scream. I notice the buzz in my legs before a big event. I feel the grip in my throat when I'm holding back something that needs to be said. I've learned to track the way my breath moves in and out of my body. And I've started to notice the thoughts that come with it. Not always loud, not always obvious, but there, just beneath the surface. The old fears and the self-doubt. The quiet assumptions that I'm not ready, not safe, not enough.

Most of the time, I wasn't even aware they were there. They ran automatically, like background noise. But now I try to meet them with curiosity instead of letting them run the show. Because once you notice the pattern, you can begin to change it.

So the next time you feel that wave coming, whether it is a restlessness, a tightness, or just a sense that something is off, pause. You do not need to analyse it or fix it. Just place your hand over your chest. Or your belly. Somewhere you can feel your own warmth.

Ask gently, *What are you trying to tell me?*

Sometimes the answer will come in words. Sometimes it will be a memory, a subtle shift in energy, or a quiet knowing in your gut. It might not make perfect sense at first, and that is okay. You do not have to believe everything that surfaces, but you can still meet it with compassion. The point is not to have the answer. The point is to stay. To remain present with yourself, even when the feeling is uncomfortable. Even when the mind wants to run. That presence is what begins to untangle the fear from the sensation. That presence is what brings you back.

This is the language of real confidence, the kind that listens and remains. Because when you begin to listen, truly listen, you realise your body was never the problem. It was never trying to betray you. It was trying to bring you back to yourself.

Silence Isn't Emptiness; It's Intelligence

So many of us have been conditioned to believe confidence has to be loud. That it needs to push forward, fill space, or prove something. But some of the most powerful moments in my life have unfolded in stillness.

In the silence of stillness, there is nothing to achieve. No role to play. No version of yourself to project. The quiet doesn't demand that you be better or different. It simply invites you to stay awhile. To sit in your own company, without rushing to escape it. Even when it feels unfamiliar.

The next time the noise around you fades, or the noise within you settles, I want you to pay attention to what surfaces. Let your shoulders soften. Let your breath return to its natural rhythm.

Stillness is not something you have to earn. It isn't a prize for being productive or getting everything right. It's a place you're already allowed to enter. A space that belongs to you, whether you've been there recently or not.

Because confidence doesn't always arrive through action. Sometimes it grows in the quiet, in the space between doing and being. And silence, real silence, is not empty at all. It's the place where you meet yourself again.

Confidence Is a Posture, Not a Performance

One morning before a speaking event, I could feel the spiral starting. That familiar pit in my stomach, the electric buzz in my chest, the quiet internal whisper saying, *You don't belong here.* I didn't have time to rewire my mindset or run through affirmations. But I had a moment, a breath and a choice.

So I stood still. I grounded both feet into the floor. I rolled my shoulders back and softened my jaw. I let my awareness drop out of my head and into my body. I breathed, not a shallow, performative breath, but a full, deliberate one. The kind that tells your nervous system: *You are here, you are safe, you don't need to rush through this moment.*

I didn't feel invincible. But I did feel present. And in that stillness, something shifted. I wasn't waiting for confidence to arrive. I was already inside it. That one breath, that one shift in posture, was enough to steady me.

Being grounded and feeling present, that's what makes the difference. It's not about feeling certain or fearless. It's about being willing to stand where you are, without collapsing into the old story that says you shouldn't be here. Confidence lives in that decision: to stay, to feel, and to ground. So let's slow it down. Try it now.

Sit or stand upright. Not stiff, just supported. Let your shoulders drop gently. Release the grip in your jaw. Unclench your hands. Bring your awareness to your feet or to the seat beneath you. Let your breath enter as if it belongs. Let it leave without effort. Feel yourself here, now, in this body. Breathing like you matter.

You don't need to speak louder or feel pressured to fill the space. Quiet Confidence often starts in silence and stillness, in the posture of a person who has decided not to leave themselves behind.

This is embodied self-trust. You are not pretending, and you are not pushing through. You are remembering something deeper. Calm does not mean fear is gone; it means you are present. Even if your heart is racing. Even if your voice trembles. Even if the room feels bigger than you, you can still take one conscious breath and anchor yourself to this moment. That breath is a message: *I am here. I belong. I do not need to earn my right to exist.*

Key Takeaways from Chapter Ten

- **Your body is not the enemy.** Its responses are protective, not shameful. Messages shaped by what it once had to survive.
- **Anxiety is memory held in sensation.** Your body remembers how something felt, often before your mind can explain it.
- **Survival patterns are learned, not fixed.** What once kept you safe can be gently unlearned as you create new experiences of safety.
- **Anchors link emotion to memory in powerful, lasting ways.** That tightness in your chest or sudden wave of emotion isn't random, it's a sign that your body remembers more than your mind realises.
- **Calm doesn't need to be earned.** You're allowed to feel peace, even if the list isn't finished, even if the world is still noisy around you.
- **Confidence is built in small moments.** It grows when you meet your body with kindness and stay present through discomfort.
- **Stillness is not emptiness, it's wisdom.** In quiet moments, your body begins to show you what's real, without the noise of performance or pressure.
- **You can rewrite the story your body carries.** The past may be etched into your nervous system, but it doesn't have to define the way you live today.

Chapter 11

The Storm Inside

"You can't stop the waves, but you can learn to surf."

— *Jon Kabat-Zinn*

You know the feeling. The sudden rush of heat to your chest. The breath that won't deepen. The mind that accelerates without your permission, rehearsing scenarios that haven't even happened yet. Maybe it started with a strange look, an awkward pause, or a message left on 'read.' Maybe it came from nowhere. But now, you're in it. The storm has arrived.

Sometimes it's a quiet build-up, like distant thunder rumbling through a conversation that didn't land quite right. Other times it hits hard and fast with no warning, no logic, just lightning in your veins. You scramble for control, for safety, for something to hold onto that might still make sense.

And all the while, your body believes it's under siege. Let's be honest: the worst storms are never the ones outside of you. They're the ones inside your chest. And those storms aren't about weather. They're about control, or more accurately, the desperate, aching, futile attempt to hold onto things that were never ours to control in the first place.

The Storm You Can't Stop

We've all learned to chase control like it's a lifeline.

If I could just say the right thing...

If I could predict what they'll do...

If I could be good enough, calm enough, smart enough...

Then maybe the storm won't come.

But storms come anyway, because the storm isn't out there; it's in here. It's the part of you that panics in uncertainty, the part that equates safety with certainty and fear with any unknown. But what if the real power isn't in stopping the storm? What if it's in learning how to stand inside it?

When the Storm Came for Me

I grew up in North Queensland, where cyclones weren't a metaphor. They were reality. Every year, the sky would shift and we'd wait. Tape the windows. Stock the cupboards. Pray the worst would pass.

In 2006, Cyclone Larry was barrelling straight toward my hometown. I was over 1,700 kilometres away at university. I was safe, but useless. I called home.

"Mum, what's happening?"

Her voice was calm, but her silence between words was louder. "The winds are picking up. We've done all we can. Now, we wait."

That's the part no one talks about:

The *waiting*. The part between preparation and impact. Where your mind has nothing to do but run. And it did.

What if they lose the house?

What if they lose power?

What if I lose them?

I wasn't in the storm. I was *becoming* it. Because that's what anxiety does. It doesn't wait for evidence. It fills in the gaps with catastrophe. It doesn't need facts. It just needs space to spin.

Hours later, another call came:

"We think we're in the eye. It's suddenly quiet."

I'll never forget that line. Because the eye of a cyclone is one of the most disorienting experiences you can imagine. Eerie, still and haunting. A strange kind of silence that doesn't feel peaceful. It feels loaded because you know it's not over. The other side is still coming.

But here's what struck me: Even in the middle of chaos, there is a place of calm. It's not after the storm, it's inside it. In finding that place, the storm loses its power.

The Real Storm

If you've ever had a panic attack, or found yourself spiralling after a throwaway comment, or completely unravelled by something seemingly small, then you know the storm I'm talking about. The outside trigger might be tiny. A glance. A shift in tone. A pause in the conversation that suddenly feels too long.

But inside, it's a cyclone (or a hurricane, depending on where in the world you live). A full-force surge of emotion with no warning and nowhere to hide. You try to act normal. You nod, smile, and keep up the conversation. But underneath the surface, your nervous system is staging a full-blown rebellion.

Your mind whispers, *You're not enough.* Your chest tightens like it's holding a secret. Your stomach flips. Your thoughts scatter. And the scariest part? You want to run... but you can't name what from. It feels like you're trying to escape yourself.

That's where the loop begins. We try to solve the discomfort by fixing the outside. We comb through the conversation, searching for clues. We try to pre-empt the fallout, read minds, and play it safe. We grip tighter. We think if we just perform better, prepare more, be more, then maybe the storm will pass. But it doesn't. Because the storm was never out there. Not really.

The real storm is what starts inside when we doubt our ability to hold ourselves through the moment. When we believe we're too fragile to stay. That's what makes the wind howl louder. That's what fuels the spiral. Chaos of the mind is inevitable, but control is possible.

Here's something you won't hear in the emergency broadcasts: the storm isn't yours to control. The control exists in how you respond, that's where your power lives.

The Eye Was Always Inside You

You might think calm is something you earn once you've solved the problem, said the perfect thing, or fixed every last detail. But the truth is quieter than that and It's braver, too. Because sometimes the most radical thing you can do in the middle of anxiety isn't to push through or figure it out. It's to pause.

To stop spiralling long enough to ask yourself a different question:

Where am I placing my power?

If you're like most of us, your attention has been hijacked and dragged into other people's reactions, into imaginary futures, into worst-case scenarios you'll probably never live through. Your nervous system reacts as if it's already happening.

But what if stillness isn't the absence of chaos; what if it's your ability to remain grounded *while* the chaos spins?

Just like in the eye of a cyclone, there is calm. It doesn't mean the storm disappears; it means you don't disappear with it.

And when you stop trying to control what you were never meant to control, like other people's thoughts, outcomes, or timing, you reclaim the one thing you can: *your response.*

This is the locus of control, not in theory, but in action. It's choosing not to feed the storm. It's noticing the pull of panic and saying to yourself, *Not today. I'm staying with myself.*

It's placing your feet on the ground and remembering: *I don't have to have all the answers to breathe.*

And every time you choose that stillness, especially when it feels impossible, you prove to yourself that the storm has less power than you thought.

Exercise: Recognising the Inner Storm

Let's make this real. Take a moment to reflect:

- When was the last time your inner storm took over?
- What triggered it?
- What story did your mind start spinning?
- What did your body do in response?
- What would it have felt like to step into the calm of the eye?
- What could I have told myself in that moment that would have helped me stay?

Write your answers down without the need to censor. The words don't have to be perfect, they just have to be true.

Your Calm Command Kit

No one walks into a cyclone unprepared. You don't wait until the roof rattles or the sky turns black to wonder where the candles are. You get ready *before* the winds arrive. Your mind deserves the same kind of preparation.

Because when you're in the grip of anxiety, it's almost impossible to *think* clearly, let alone remember the tools that might help. That's why we build your Calm Command Kit now, not in the middle of the storm.

This isn't a toolbox for perfection. It's a sanctuary for when things get messy. and a quiet declaration: *I know who I am, even when fear gets loud.*

Here's what goes inside:

Focus: Your flashlight.

Anxiety thrives in scattered attention. So in the moment, ask yourself: *Where is my focus right now?* Bring it back, whether that be to your breath, your feet, or the feeling of your clothes against your skin. Whatever anchors you to *now*. Because fear can only grow where focus goes, and you get to choose where that is.

Breath and sound: Your anchors.

Play a grounding playlist or put on a calming podcast. Simply breathe in for four, hold for four, and exhale for four. These aren't just techniques; they're signals to your nervous system: *It's okay to calm down now.* You don't have to feel calm yet. Just breathe like someone who could.

Support: Your shelter.

Who do you call when your world shakes? Whose words help you remember your strength when you forget? Make a list. Keep it somewhere you'll see it when everything feels like too much. You don't have to face the storm alone.

Stillness practices: Your medicine.

This isn't about clearing your mind or sitting cross-legged on a mountaintop. Stillness might be a walk, a yawn, or a few minutes lying on the floor with your hand on your chest. It's anything that says to your body, *I'm not in danger now*. Over time, this becomes a pattern your body learns to trust.

Exercise: Build Your Kit

Take a breath. Let's explore what supports you.

- What helps bring your focus back to now, when your thoughts start to scatter?
- What sounds soothe your system and help you exhale?
- Who reminds you of your strength when the ground feels unsteady?
- What small stillness practices help your body feel safe and settled?

Write your answers down. Put them somewhere visible: your phone, your mirror, the notes app you always forget to open.

The storm will come. But when it does, you won't have to figure everything out. You'll already be ready.

The Darkest Hour

Close your eyes and picture this clearly. This isn't a fantasy, it's a future memory already beginning to form.

You step into a moment that would have once unravelled you. Maybe it's a crowded room where all eyes could land on you. Maybe it's a conversation where your truth needs to be spoken aloud. Maybe it's a decision you've delayed for years, now waiting for you to make it. In the past, your breath might have quickened, your thoughts might have spun, your chest might have tightened. But not this time.

This time, your feet are on the ground. Your breath is in your body. You are here. And you are not bracing. You are not shrinking into silence, not replaying every possible outcome, not preparing to run. Something within you feels steady. The storm is still there, but this time, you are not caught in it. You are the eye. The calm centre. The place the chaos can't reach.

The noise around you may rise. The fear may whisper its old, familiar lines. The world may spin, throw distractions, invite you back into the pattern. But you stay rooted. You stay with yourself. Not frozen, not passive, but anchored in something deeper. You've made contact with the part of you that no longer sees fear as a command, but as a cue to breathe even deeper.

You're not chasing perfection. You're not trying to silence every doubt. You're simply meeting the moment with something real.

Quiet Confidence

You're choosing not to abandon yourself. That's the shift. That's the power.

Because now, you remember what you had forgotten. The storm was never you. It may have surrounded you. It may have shaken you. It may have swept you off your feet a thousand times. But it never was you. You are not the panic. You are not the noise. You are not the moment you lost your words or forgot your strength. You are the one who kept returning. The one who stayed. The one who dared to learn a new way to move through it all.

And now, you do not need to prove yourself through noise. You do not need to earn your place with performance. You are allowed to stand here, quietly, yet confidently. You are allowed to show up as you are, without explanation or apology. Because this time, you know. You know who you are. You know what matters. And you know how to come back to calm, even when the world doesn't offer it.

So take this image. Let it settle in your body. Let it anchor you in moments when the doubt returns. You don't have to roar to be powerful. You don't have to push to be worthy. You can meet the moment with softness and stillness, and still be unshakable.

Because now, finally, you own the calm.

Key Takeaways from Chapter Eleven

- **The real storm begins within.** Racing thoughts or a pounding heart aren't flaws; they're signs your nervous system is seeking safety.
- **Control is not the cure.** Trying to fix everything outside only fuels the panic within. Calm begins by turning inward.
- **There is a quiet centre within you.** Even when everything spins, you can return to that steady place and stop following fear.
- **Anxiety is not your fault.** It's your nervous system doing what it learned to do, and with support, that pattern can change.
- **Stillness is your birthright.** You don't need to earn peace. You just need to pause long enough to feel the ground beneath you.
- **Calm is not the opposite of chaos.** It's the strength to stay rooted while the world moves around you.
- **Safety starts in the body.** Simple anchors like music, breath, and connection teach your system it no longer has to brace for impact.
- **Rituals are not overreactions.** They're how you show your nervous system that you're prepared, not panicked.
- **Fear may still visit, but it doesn't have to lead.** Even when it shows up, you can return to your tools, your choices, and the steadiness you've built.

Chapter 12

Returning with New Sight

"He who returns from a journey is not the same as he who left."

— *Chinese proverb*

It's not until you walk over ground you've walked over a million times that you realise you are seeing it differently now. The once-familiar world is no longer ordinary because you are no longer the same person. Your old lens has been shattered. The automatic, unconscious way you used to operate is gone. You've rewritten the script and stepped into someone real, grounded, and awake. And as you embrace this new identity, something profound happens. When you see yourself with new eyes, others start to see you differently too.

After the Storm

When the storm finally passes, calm returns, but everything is changed. In its wake, you survey the wreckage. At first, you see the destruction, the loss, the unfamiliar landscape left behind. But then you realise that the storm didn't destroy you. It cleared the path. It stripped away the illusions, the false narratives, and the self-imposed limitations that kept you small. What looked like devastation was actually *transformation*.

Now, standing on fresh ground, you have something you've never had before: *choice*. A clean slate. A blank page. The power to build something new, something *intentional*.

I reflect on my own storm and the version of myself who once looked in the mirror, confused, uncertain, unsure of who was staring back. That boy, burdened by shyness, convinced he wasn't enough, is still part of me. But I no longer believe his story. Because the person standing in front of the mirror today has *proof*. Proof that Quiet Confidence dominates over doubt. Proof that the mind that once kept me trapped has now set me free. And for that, I am *eternally* grateful.

Gratitude, My Secret Sauce

Gratitude is the secret ingredient that makes life richer. I've learned to be grateful for my life, including the shyness, the self-doubt, and the emergence of Quiet Confidence. I'm even grateful for the struggle, because without the tension, there would be no transformation. Without contrast, there is no hero's journey. Life would flatten into a straight line, and I've walked that path before. Uncomfortable comfort isn't comfort at all. Without the journey, this book wouldn't exist. And you wouldn't be here, reading these words.

I used to fear putting myself out there, afraid of criticism, rejection, and failure. Now I'm grateful for every challenge, every moment of discomfort, and every lesson. I say that because they made me *who I am*.

I used to worry about what people would think of me. Now? I'm grateful that I have a voice at all. That I have the courage to use it. And if someone throws a tomato my way? I'll make tomato sauce. And I'll be grateful for the opportunity.

Three Generations

I think back to the child I was. A boy who felt like an outsider, a misfit, an anomaly. Someone who believed he was the *only one* who felt this way.

He never considered that maybe, just maybe, he wasn't alone.

And then I look back further at my father and my grandfather. At the *pattern* I never saw before.

For years, I believed my struggles with shyness were unique to me. Then I discovered that my grandfather, William Edward (Ted) Annesley, carried the same quiet nature. Ted was a fisherman, a husband, a father of three boys. A quiet achiever, a man of wisdom and deep thought, someone who understood the world through observation rather than dominance. He spent hours in his fishing boat, at one with the water, the tides, the rhythms of nature.

He was a *listener*. A *thinker*. A natural counsellor, with a calming presence that others relied on. He never rushed decisions. Everything was deliberate, well-planned and carefully considered.

One of his greatest projects was building a boat by hand. First, he carved a small model. He meticulously designed every piece before attempting the real thing. He tested. He planned. He refined. And when the time came to build the full-scale version, he was ready.

Except for one thing. The clamps holding the frame were too tight, and the wood buckled under pressure. A setback that could have sent someone else into frustration, into defeat. But not Ted. He didn't see failure. He saw *adjustment*.

He recalibrated, reworked, and persisted. The result? A beautifully crafted boat that was strong, balanced, and built to glide effortlessly across the water. And that was Ted. Measured. Patient. Persistent.

He taught his children the same lessons. *Never be in a rush. Measure twice, cut once.* And when faced with bullies? His advice was simple: *If you lose your temper, you lose control.*

But for all his wisdom, there was something he never taught us because he never got the chance to learn it for himself. Ted spent his life putting everyone else first. He worked hard, provided, and planned for the future. But when his health failed him in his early fifties, and the doctor delivered the diagnosis of cancer, he was forced to face a devastating truth.

He had postponed *living*. He never took the trips he dreamed of. Never gave himself permission to put his own desires first. He had *waited*. And now, he had run out of time.

In his final months, the quiet patience that defined him was replaced by something else: anger, resentment, a sense of *incompleteness*. And I can't help but wonder, was he angry because he had spent too much time *holding back*? Had he silenced himself one too many times? Did he carry words, desires, dreams that he never gave himself the chance to say out loud? I think about that a lot, and so does my father, Anthony.

Breaking the Cycle

My father and I share many of Ted's traits. We, too, have been labelled "the quiet ones." We, too, have struggled to balance thoughtfulness with the need to *speak up*. And we, too, have had moments where we held back, not out of a lack of ideas, but out of a habit so ingrained it felt like second nature.

But unlike Ted, my father was given a front-row seat to what regret looks like. He watched his father hold back until it was too late. He saw how years of silence can turn into frustration, how unspoken thoughts and unpursued dreams can weigh a person down.

And because of that, he made a decision. He would not let history repeat itself. He vowed to live differently. He was committed to taking the trips, to *speak up*, to live without waiting for the "perfect" moment. And because of that decision, he set in motion a ripple effect. His decision gave *me* permission to do the same.

I realised that Quiet Confidence started with Ted but it wouldn't end with him. My father and I are carrying forward what he never could. We are breaking the cycle. We are reclaiming the parts of ourselves that were once buried under shyness, and we are choosing to live fully, unapologetically, *now*.

We've made a pact. No more carrying regret to the grave. Only lessons, love, and the courage to live fully while we can.

Returning Home

Some time ago, I returned to the place of my childhood, my ordinary world. The place where I once wrote those quiet, damaging labels. The place where shyness first took root. I walked the same streets, touched the same walls, as if I were following breadcrumbs I didn't know I'd left.

I rummaged through old boxes, unearthing photos and school papers I hadn't seen in years. Faded edges, scribbled notes, fragments of a self I had outgrown but never quite confronted.

The evidence was there: reports, remarks, and reflections describing a shy, reserved, hesitant child. And I didn't flinch. Because that label no longer defines me. I've made peace with it. I understand now that it was a reflection of who I *felt* I had to be, not who I truly was.

But then, I turned the first page of my Year Two report card. And there it was:

"Joel is quietly confident."

I froze. It was a truth I had missed. A seed planted long before I ever realised I needed to water it. A label I once overlooked that I now fully claimed.

I returned to my childhood home with new sight. The creek beds where my imagination once ran wild. The trees that stood sentinel as I grew. Everything was the same. But everything had changed. Because *I* had changed. I no longer needed to shrink. I no longer carried the weight of those old, misunderstood labels. I no longer saw myself through the eyes of the boy who believed he was awkwardly different.

I saw with clarity. With compassion. With truth. There was never anything wrong with me. I wasn't strange or lacking or somehow on the outside of life. I had simply forgotten. Forgotten how to trust my own pace. Forgotten that quiet was never the problem; it was the misunderstanding of it. I spent years trying to fix something that didn't need fixing. And all along, the strength I was searching for was already within me, waiting to be seen. I wasn't lost. I was becoming. And now, I remember who I am. I am quietly confident.

Your Legacy

There's so much pressure these days to define it all. Your mission. Your purpose. Your legacy. As if you're supposed to carve it into stone before you've even lived it. But what if they're not the same thing? What if they were never meant to be?

A mission is something you can stand for. It's the direction you choose to walk in. It can be bold, brave, world-changing, or quiet, grounded, and personal. Your purpose? That's where so many people get lost. Trying to find the one perfect answer, the one true calling, as if it's hiding somewhere, waiting to be unlocked. But your purpose doesn't have to be a headline. Sometimes it's as simple as following what feels honest. What brings peace. What lights something up in you, even when life feels heavy.

And legacy... legacy is something else entirely. It's not something you control. It's not a statement you make; it's the echo you leave behind. It's the warmth someone feels after talking to you. The courage someone finds after watching you take a step. It's the energy that lingers in a room after you've gone. Legacy is what happens when the small things add up. It's not what you count; it's what you carry. And what you pass on.

I used to think I had to define my legacy, give it a name, a number, a measurable outcome. Something that made sense on a vision board. But now I know: legacy is fluid. It's not a finish line. It's a living thing that grows with you. I hope mine never stops evolving because I'm still becoming. And so are you.

You don't need a perfect mission statement. You don't need to figure out your whole life in one sitting. You're allowed to exhale. To soften. To trust that showing up matters. That your presence makes an impact. That the way you speak to yourself, the way you treat others, the way you return to yourself after hardship—that's legacy.

And if you've experienced anxiety, that doesn't mean there's something wrong with you. It means you feel something. And feeling something, anything, is what connects you to this life. It means you're alive. And if you can feel fear, doubt, or discomfort, then you also have the capacity to feel joy, peace, connection, and love. All of it belongs. All of it is human.

Some emotions need to be felt all the way through, not ignored. Not replaced with "positive vibes only," but honoured. Because when you feel fully, you live fully. And when you get stuck in old thought patterns, here's the quiet truth: you don't have to stay there.

You always have the power to choose a new response. And maybe that's the most meaningful legacy of all.

Key Takeaways from Chapter Eleven

- **Transformation is quiet, but undeniable.** Sometimes, simply walking through the same place with new eyes is enough to realise you've changed.
- **The storm didn't break you, it revealed you.** What felt like chaos cleared the noise and left you with strength, clarity, and choice.
- **Shyness isn't just personal, it can be generational.** You may be carrying patterns that started long before you. But you don't have to carry them forever.
- **Gratitude reframes everything.** You can fear failure, or you can be grateful for growth. The moment you stop resisting discomfort and start thanking it, even your struggles become sacred.
- **Your legacy isn't a number, it's a ripple.** Legacy isn't fixed or flashy. It's the quiet impact you make through how you live, how you love, and how you show up. Let it evolve with you.
- **You were never lost, only disconnected.** Reflection and self-trust help you rewrite the story, freeing you from what once defined you. The truth was always there, waiting to be remembered.

Chapter 13

The Breakup That Changed Everything

"There are moments in life when the person you used to be meets the person you've become."

— *From the Author's Note*

I didn't write this book because I had all the answers. I wrote it because I needed to. Because there was a version of me still carrying the weight of old labels. A version who believed that shyness was just who I was. A version who longed to be seen but was terrified of being visible.

And if I'm honest, I still carry him to some degree, not with shame, but with tenderness. He walks beside me now, no longer calling the shots, but never forgotten.

That's the real story here. It wasn't a perfect transformation, but it was a powerful one. One where I stopped treating shyness as the enemy and began to understand it for what it truly was: *a pattern*. A habit of protection. A way of staying safe in a world that sometimes felt too loud. But I've outgrown it. And I no longer see the past as something to shut out or escape from. I see it now as something I can stand beside, acknowledge, honour, and grow beyond. That's what this is: a quiet, grounded choice to meet the future with open eyes.

This Is the Goodbye

There was a time I believed I had to cut parts of myself away to feel free. That if I could bury the quiet parts, silence the hesitations, and deny what made me feel different, I might finally become confident. But the truth is, you don't grow by erasing who you've been. You grow by seeing yourself clearly, by understanding your patterns, and by choosing something new: lovingly, consciously, without shame.

This isn't a dramatic ending. It's not a rejection. It's an honest turning point. A quiet, steady decision to live differently now. To meet myself with more compassion. To lead with more presence. To stop shrinking for the comfort of others and finally step fully into who I've been becoming all along.

And the beautiful part? I can say this with clarity now; I like who I'm becoming. I'm proud of him.

The Shift Is Permanent, Even in the Doubt

There comes a moment when clarity arrives not as a whisper, but as a flash of lightning, brief, illuminating, impossible to ignore.

Quiet Confidence

That's what this journey gave me. Not just the courage to share my story, but the perspective to truly see it for the first time. It was like sitting in the optometrist's chair after years of blurred edges, trying lens after lens, squinting at the same fuzzy lines. "Is it clearer now? How about now?" And then suddenly, yes. That's it. That's the one. And once you see yourself clearly, you cannot unsee.

You can't pretend you're small when you've glimpsed the size of your strength. You can't believe you're faulty when you've remembered how whole you already are. What I see now isn't someone to fix, but someone in motion. And that, more than anything, has changed everything.

Yes, there will still be days when doubt returns. Not as a failure, but as a flicker; an echo of who you used to be. You might be walking through the shops, not thinking about much, when a song plays that takes you somewhere you didn't expect to go. A memory rises, a feeling stirs, and for a moment, the world feels heavy again. You might find yourself pulling back, instinctively shrinking, as if invisibility might offer safety. But now, something is different. You notice the shift. You take a moment to pause. You breathe with intention. You remind yourself of what you now know: this is a pattern, not a truth. A shadow, not your shape.

And in that moment, you choose to stay steady. The world around you might still be spinning, the noise still rising, but something within you has shifted. That is what Quiet Confidence truly is; not the disappearance of fear or overwhelm, but the presence of something deeper.

It is the strength to meet discomfort with calm, the willingness to stay present when it would be easier to retreat. It is the quiet ability to return to yourself, to breathe deeply, to move gently, even when uncertainty lingers. You no longer feel the need to explain your fear away or wait until everything is perfect. You simply stand, as you are, because you trust yourself enough to stay.

Integration, Not Erasure

The biggest shift of all wasn't about eliminating shyness or pretending I'd outgrown every trace of it. It was the realisation that I never needed to delete the shy version of me in the first place. He's still here, gently woven into my story, not as a flaw, but as a foundation. He's the one who taught me to pause, to notice, to observe deeply and speak with intention.

He's the one who helped me find meaning in quiet corners and stillness in noisy rooms. He learned how to survive with grace when the world felt too loud, and for that, I'll always thank him. But he doesn't lead anymore. He rides in the backseat now, while I, fully present, grounded, and whole, have taken the wheel. This isn't a story of exile. It's a story of integration. Because the moment you stop judging who you were, you create the freedom to become who you truly are.

Your Quiet Confidence

Maybe this book found you in a moment when you needed to hear something different. Maybe you recognised yourself in these pages: the tension between wanting to be seen and fearing the spotlight, the quiet tug-of-war between hiding and hoping someone might understand. Maybe, like me, you've begun to notice the old patterns not as flaws to erase, but as signals that you're ready for something more.

And maybe now, for the first time in a long time, you see something new taking shape. This isn't the end. This is a quiet beginning. You've broken up with shyness, not by disowning your past, but by stepping into a new kind of self-respect. You've softened the voice of self-doubt, not by pretending it was never there, but by choosing to respond differently. You've started to come home to yourself in the most profound and grounded way.

Now, you get to walk into the world with presence. You move with steadiness, grounded in who you are, guided by your Quiet Confidence. Not loud. Not seeking applause. Simply real.

And before we close this chapter, there's someone I need to speak to one last time, the part of me I once believed I had to hide.

Joel Annesley

Dear Shyness,

You were there when the world felt too loud, too fast, too uncertain. You stepped in when I didn't yet have the words. You kept me quiet when silence felt safer than being seen.

And for that, I thank you.

You were never the enemy. You were the protector. But somewhere along the way, that protection became a cage.

The longer I let you lead, the smaller I became.

I used to blame you. I used to feel like I was your hostage. I was embarrassed and ashamed by you.

Now, I honour you. You helped me survive.

But I've grown. And I'm ready to lead myself. You'll always be a part of me, just not the part in charge. This book began as a letter to the part of me still learning how to believe.

And it ends with this:

Thank you. I'm ready now.

With love,

Joel

The Quiet Confidence Manifesto

I am no longer waiting for permission. I do not need to be more, do more, or prove myself to be worthy of taking up space. I am already enough.

Shyness is no longer my identity. It was a chapter, not my story. I have nothing to apologise for, nothing to shrink away from. My voice matters. My presence matters. And I choose to step forward, not fade into the background.

I trust myself. I trust that I can handle whatever comes my way, even when my hands shake, even when my voice wavers. I will not let fear dictate my choices. Instead, I choose courage. Quietly, yet confidently.

I do not measure my worth by how loud I am or how perfectly I perform. I embrace the power of being intentional, of speaking with conviction, of leading in my own way.

I am not here to please everyone. Not everyone will understand me, and that's okay. I release the need for approval. I am building my life on my own terms.

I am stepping into the world with Quiet Confidence. Not forced, not faked, just real, unwavering belief in who I am.

And now, it's your turn.

You are ready. You have always been ready. You have everything you need. Shyness is your past. Leave it behind and keep walking forward.

Your next chapter begins with courage.

RESOURCES AND SUPPORT

If something stirred in you as you read, a quiet yes, an exhale, a sense of coming home, trust that. The journey doesn't end here. It deepens with practice, support, and reminders that you don't have to return to old patterns just because they're familiar. This is your invitation to keep going, gently and intentionally.

Quiet Confidence Starter Guide (Free Download)

A journaling companion to support your inner work. This guide will help you meet yourself with kindness, explore what's beneath the surface, and gently guide you back to self-trust, one insight at a time.

Download at:

joelannesley.com/quietconfidencestarterguide

Quiet Confidence Workbook (Buy the Hardcopy)

Want to go deeper? The workbook expands on the ideas in this book with space to write, reflect, and personalise your journey. It's a beautifully designed tool to support your growth beyond the page.

Order your copy at:

joelannesley.com/quietconfidenceworkbook

Coaching, Courses and Clinical Support

Whether you're looking for therapeutic support, community-based coaching, or self-paced learning, there's a next step that's right for you. I work with thoughtful, sensitive, deep-feeling humans who are ready to live with greater self-trust and Quiet Confidence.

Explore your options at:

joelannesley.com

FURTHER READING & INSPIRATIONS

The journey to Quiet Confidence was never mine alone. These works, authors, and studies have shaped the foundation of this book. If something sparked your curiosity or opened a new doorway, you may find deeper insight in the pages below.

- **Dr. Candace Pert**, *Molecules of Emotion* – A groundbreaking look at how the body stores emotion, shaping our physical and mental health.
- **Dr. Bessel van der Kolk**, *The Body Keeps the Score* – A powerful exploration of trauma, memory, and healing through the nervous system.
- **Dr. Kristin Neff**, *Self-Compassion* – A transformative approach to replacing harsh self-talk with true inner kindness.
- **Susan Cain**, *Quiet* – A celebration of introversion that inspired millions to see their quiet nature as a strength, not a flaw.
- **Dr. Joe Dispenza**, *Breaking the Habit of Being Yourself* – Blending neuroscience and meditation to rewire how we relate to our thoughts and patterns.
- **Jon Kabat-Zinn**, *Wherever You Go, There You Are* – A meditation guide that returns us to presence, breath, and the simplicity of now.
- **Peter Levine**, *Waking the Tiger* – A somatic lens into how trauma shapes the body and how we can release it gently.

Further Reading & Inspirations

- **Brianna Wiest,** *The Mountain Is You* – A moving exploration of self-sabotage, healing, and stepping into the life you're meant to live.
- **James Clear**, *Atomic Habits* – For understanding the tiny shifts that create big, lasting change over time.
- **Dr. Michael Yapko** – His many books on hypnosis and psychotherapy offer a clear, compassionate understanding of anxiety, depression, and the learned patterns that shape our emotional lives.
- **Gordon Young** – Creator of the Gordian Therapy model of Psychotherapy, a practical framework for understanding how anxiety, fears, phobias, and other psychological patterns form and persist. His insights and teachings have deeply shaped my therapeutic approach.

About the Author

Joel Annesley is a confidence coach, clinical hypnotherapist, and author of *Quiet Confidence*. His motto: Master Your Mind. Command Your Voice. Drawing from his own journey of overcoming shyness and self-doubt, he helps introverts, overthinkers, and professionals develop unshakable confidence and master their presence. Combining NLP, solution-focused coaching, and clinical hypnotherapy, Joel delivers real-world strategies to silence anxiety, rewire self-doubt, and communicate with confidence.

Joel runs a therapy clinic in Sydney, providing clinical hypnotherapy, while also working with clients worldwide through coaching programs, books, and online resources, helping them take control of their inner dialogue and step into their full potential.

Learn More About the Author:

www.joelannesley.com

www.ingramcontent.com/pod-product-compliance
Lightning Source LLC
Chambersburg PA
CBHW020533080526
44583CB00013B/845